# Journey To Marrakech

## Discovering the Secrets of Morocco's Ancient City

Alfred Reed

All rights reserved. No part of this publication may be reproduced, distributed, or transmitted in any form or by any means, including photocopying, recording, or other electronic or mechanical methods, without the prior written permission of the publisher, except in the case of brief quotations embodied in critical reviews and certain other noncommercial uses permitted by copyright law Copyright© (Alfred Reed)

**Introduction** .................................................................................... 4
    Welcome to Marrakech: A City of Contrasts ..................... 4
    A Brief History and Overview ........................................... 5
    How to Use This Guide ..................................................... 8

**A Glimpse into the Past** ...................................................... 12
    The Founding of Marrakech ............................................. 12
    Key Historical Periods and Dynasties ............................. 14
    Marrakech in Modern Times ............................................ 18

**Arriving in Marrakech** ........................................................ 23
    Transportation: Flights and Getting Around ................... 23
    Understanding Local Customs and Etiquette .................. 28
    Essential Travel Tips for First-Time Visitors .................. 34

**Exploring the Medina** ......................................................... 42
    Jemaa el-Fnaa: The Heart of Marrakech ......................... 42
    Navigating the Souks Shopping for Spices, Textiles, and Crafts ................................................................................ 48
    Key Landmarks Koutoubia Mosque, Ben Youssef Madrasa, and Saadian Tombs ........................................ 56

**Marrakech's Architectural Wonders** ................................ 62
    Bahia Palace: A Glimpse into Moroccan Royalty ... 62
    El Badi Palace Ruins of a Majestic Past ........................ 67
    The Majestic Riads of Marrakech ................................... 72

**Gardens and Green Spaces** ................................................ 79
    Menara Gardens Serenity at the Foot of the Atlas Mountains ............................................................................ 85

**Culinary Delights** ................................................................. 91
    Traditional Moroccan Dishes to Try ............................... 91
    The Best Restaurants and Street Food Spots ........ 97

Moroccan Tea Culture and Café Scene................ 104

**Art and Culture..........................................................111**

Museums and Galleries: Marrakech Museum, Maison de la Photographie......................................111

Traditional Arts and Crafts Carpets, Pottery, and Jewelry.................................................................... 115

Festivals and Cultural Events: When to Visit for Special Occasions................................................. 129

The Modern Side of Marrakech............................ 136

Shopping Beyond the Medina: Boutiques and Designer Stores..................................................... 142

**Day Trips and Excursions..........................................150**

Atlas Mountains: Hiking and Outdoor Adventures 150

Contemporary Art and Fashion in Marrakech....... 150

The Agafay Desert: A Taste of the Sahara........... 158

Visiting Essaouira: The Windy City by the Sea..... 163

**Wellness and Relaxation............................................170**

Hammams: Experiencing Moroccan Baths........... 170

Spa and Wellness Retreats: Indulging in Luxury and Rejuvenation..........................................................178

**Staying in Marrakech..................................................187**

Riads vs. Hotels: Where to Stay........................... 187

Best Budget, Mid-range, and Luxury Accommodations................................................... 195

Best Budget, Mid-range, and Luxury Accommodations................................................... 202

Unique Stays:Camping, Villas, and Eco-Lodges.. 209

Unique Stays for Unforgettable Experiences........216

**Essential Travel Tips................................................. 224**

Navigating the City: Transportation Options and

Taxis...................................................................224
Choosing the Right Transport for Your Trip.......... 230
Safety and Scams to Avoid...................................230
Packing Essentials for Marrakech........................ 238
**A Journey to Remember............................................ 245**

# Introduction

## Welcome to Marrakech: A City of Contrasts

Marrakech is a city that captures the essence of Morocco's past and present, a place where ancient traditions blend with modern life. Known as the "Red City" for its iconic red sandstone buildings, it offers visitors a sensory experience like no other. From the vibrant colors of the markets and the hum of daily life in Medina, to the quiet, peaceful courtyards of its riads, Marrakech is full of contrasts waiting to be explored.

As you wander through the city, you'll encounter centuries-old architecture that stands alongside contemporary art galleries and stylish cafes. The call to prayer echoes through the streets, while in the newer parts of town, you'll find the sounds of modern life: buzzing scooters, lively conversations, and the clinking of coffee cups in trendy lounges.

But Marrakech is more than its sights and sounds—it's the atmosphere that draws you in. The energy is tangible, yet there's a sense of tranquility beneath it all. In the heart of the bustling souks, you'll find artisans crafting traditional goods with skills passed down through generations. At the same time, the modern side of

Marrakech, with its boutique hotels, luxury restaurants, and high-end fashion shops, shows how the city embraces change while honoring its roots.

Whether you're visiting to explore the rich history, experience the world-famous cuisine, or unwind in the hidden gardens and hammams, Marrakech offers something for everyone. This guide will take you through the city's many faces, offering a window into the past while guiding you through the present.

So, whether it's your first time here or you're returning to uncover more secrets, Marrakech is ready to welcome you with open arms. Let this book be your companion as you journey through a city that refuses to be defined by just one thing—a place where contrasts come together to create something truly unforgettable.

## A Brief History and Overview

Marrakech, one of Morocco's most captivating cities, has been a gateway between the ancient traditions of Africa and the influences of Europe and the Middle East for centuries. Founded in 1070 by the Almoravid dynasty, the city has evolved into a cultural and economic hub, earning it a prominent place in Moroccan history. But beyond its historical significance,

Marrakech's charm lies in its ability to constantly reinvent itself while staying true to its roots.

Originally established as a trading post and military outpost, Marrakech quickly grew into a bustling city due to its strategic location at the crossroads of several important trade routes. Over time, it became a center for culture, learning, and architecture, attracting scholars, craftsmen, and traders from all over the region. The influence of these different cultures is evident in the city's stunning architecture, from its towering minarets and grand palaces to the intricately decorated riads hidden within the walls of the Medina.

The city's name itself is rooted in its history. The word "Marrakech" is believed to come from the Berber words "Mur Akush," meaning "Land of God," reflecting the spiritual importance the city has held for many centuries. As one of Morocco's four imperial cities, Marrakech has been shaped by various dynasties, including the Almohads, Merinids, and Saadians, each leaving their own unique mark on the city.

One of the most iconic features of Marrakech is its distinct red hue, which has earned it the nickname "The Red City." This color comes from the local red sandstone used to build many of the city's structures, giving it a striking, almost otherworldly appearance, especially during sunset when the entire city seems to glow.

Marrakech has also served as a melting pot of cultures and ideas, thanks to its long history as a meeting point for traders, travelers, and nomads. The city's souks (markets) are a testament to this, offering a dizzying array of goods—from handwoven carpets and brass lanterns to fragrant spices and fresh mint for traditional tea. The souks themselves are a maze of alleyways, each dedicated to a specific craft or trade, reflecting Marrakech's deep artisanal traditions.

Over the centuries, Marrakech has also been a center for Islamic learning and culture, as seen in its many religious monuments, such as the Koutoubia Mosque, the largest mosque in the city. Other architectural marvels, like the Bahia Palace and the Saadian Tombs, provide a glimpse into the royal past of Marrakech, where sultans once ruled and lavishly decorated their surroundings.

In modern times, Marrakech continues to thrive, not only as a tourist destination but also as a hub for art, fashion, and gastronomy. While the ancient Medina still retains its traditional charm, newer parts of the city like Gueliz and Hivernage showcase a different side of Marrakech—one that embraces the contemporary without losing sight of its heritage.

Whether you're drawn to its rich history, the labyrinthine souks, or the luxurious riads and gardens, Marrakech offers an experience unlike any other. It's a city where every corner reveals something new, where the past meets the present, and where tradition and innovation coexist.

Marrakech remains a jewel in Morocco's crown—a city that invites exploration, whether you're fascinated by its history or enchanted by its modern energy.

## How to Use This Guide

This book is designed to be your comprehensive companion as you explore Marrakech, whether you're visiting for the first time or returning for a deeper dive into its vibrant culture. To make the most of your journey, here's how to navigate the guide and find the information that matters most to you:

**Organized by Experience**
Each chapter of this guide is tailored to help you explore a different aspect of Marrakech, from its historical landmarks and architectural wonders to its bustling markets and tranquil gardens. Whether you're interested in history, food, or shopping, you'll find chapters dedicated to each area of interest, allowing you to plan your trip around what excites you the most.

### Detailed Itineraries and Practical Tips

Throughout the book, you'll find suggested itineraries that fit different travel styles—whether you prefer a fast-paced adventure or a relaxed exploration. Practical travel tips are included in each section, such as how to navigate the city, where to eat, and what to wear depending on the season. These insights will help you feel prepared and confident as you explore Marrakech.

### Cultural Insights

To enhance your experience, this guide goes beyond surface-level recommendations and dives into the cultural, historical, and artistic significance of Marrakech. From learning about local customs and traditions to understanding the importance of certain landmarks, these insights will enrich your visit and give you a deeper connection to the city.

### Insider Recommendations

While the guide covers popular tourist attractions, it also highlights hidden gems and local favorites that aren't always featured in typical travel books. Whether it's a small family-run restaurant, an off-the-beaten-path souk, or a lesser-known garden, these insider tips will help you discover a more authentic side of Marrakech.

### Navigating the City

Marrakech is a city of contrasts, with the historic Medina and the more modern districts offering very different experiences. This guide will help you seamlessly move between the two, with tips on transportation, directions for walking tours, and suggestions on how to avoid common tourist pitfalls. Maps and directions will guide you through the maze-like streets of the Medina and ensure you get the most out of your visit to both the old and new parts of the city.

**Day Trips and Excursions**
If you're interested in exploring beyond the city limits, this guide includes a chapter on day trips and excursions. From the Atlas Mountains to the Agafay Desert, we've covered the best nearby adventures for those looking to experience the diverse landscapes surrounding Marrakech.

**Flexible Format for Every Traveler**
Whether you're planning a short stay or a longer visit, this guide is structured to allow flexibility. You can follow the chapters in order to get a comprehensive understanding of the city, or simply dip into the sections that interest you the most. Each chapter is self-contained, so you can easily skip to topics like food, architecture, or wellness without missing crucial details.

**Planning Essentials**
In the final chapters, you'll find packing lists, safety tips, and essential travel information to help you prepare for your trip. From understanding local currency and tipping

practices to packing for Marrakech's diverse climate, this section ensures you have everything you need for a smooth and enjoyable experience.

**Interactive Experiences**

Throughout the guide, you'll encounter suggestions for interactive activities, such as trying your hand at bargaining in the souks, visiting a traditional hammam, or attending a cooking class to learn the art of Moroccan cuisine. These experiences will give you a hands-on connection to the local culture and make your trip even more memorable.

# A Glimpse into the Past

## The Founding of Marrakech

Marrakech's origins date back to the 11th century, when the Almoravid dynasty established it as their capital in 1070. The Almoravids, a Berber empire, played a key role in spreading Islam across North Africa and Southern Spain. They were both warriors and scholars, and it was under their leadership that Marrakech became a thriving political and cultural center.

The location of Marrakech was carefully chosen due to its strategic importance. Nestled between the Atlas Mountains and the desert, it was ideally positioned at the crossroads of ancient trade routes. This location made it a natural hub for commerce, drawing traders from the Sahara, sub-Saharan Africa, and the Mediterranean. Over time, Marrakech grew into a bustling marketplace where gold, ivory, spices, and textiles were exchanged.

The city's name, derived from the Berber phrase "Mur Akush," meaning "Land of God," reflects its spiritual and cultural significance from the beginning. The Almoravids built the foundation of what would become one of Morocco's most important cities, starting with the construction of key landmarks, including the first mosques and fortifications.

One of the most important early projects was the creation of an intricate irrigation system known as the "khettara." This underground network of water channels allowed the city to flourish in the arid landscape, enabling the growth of lush gardens and agricultural fields. These gardens, known as "menzahs," were essential for supplying the city with fresh produce and became a symbol of prosperity.

Marrakech's distinctive red sandstone walls were also constructed during the reign of the Almoravids, giving the city its famous nickname, "The Red City." These fortifications not only provided protection but also displayed the strength and wealth of the Almoravid empire.

Over the centuries, Marrakech became a beacon of Islamic culture and learning. The Almoravids established religious schools, or "madrasas," and attracted scholars from across the Islamic world. Their successors, the Almohads, expanded on this legacy, building landmarks like the Koutoubia Mosque, which still stands as one of the city's most iconic structures.

Marrakech's early history is marked by a blend of military power, religious devotion, and cultural development. The city thrived as a center of learning, trade, and spirituality, setting the stage for its enduring legacy as one of Morocco's most important cities.

## Key Historical Periods and Dynasties

Marrakech's rich history is shaped by the influence of various dynasties, each leaving its own unique imprint on the city. From the founding Almoravids to the Saadian dynasty's golden age, these periods have woven together to make Marrakech the cultural treasure it is today. Below is an overview of the most significant dynasties that ruled Marrakech, highlighting their contributions to the city's architecture, culture, and politics.

1. The Almoravid Dynasty (1040–1147)

**Founding and Flourishing of Marrakech**

The Almoravids, a Berber Muslim dynasty, founded Marrakech in 1070 and established it as their capital. Under their rule, the city became a major political, religious, and trading center. They laid the foundations of the city by building the first mosques, walls, and the revolutionary irrigation system, "khettara," which enabled the cultivation of lush gardens.

The Almoravids were known for their devotion to Islamic learning and architecture. They brought scholars and artisans to the city, making it a center for education and religious study. Their construction of religious and public buildings set the stage for Marrakech's growth.

2. The Almohad Dynasty (1147–1269)

**Cultural Renaissance and Expansion**

The Almohads, who overthrew the Almoravids in 1147, were a reformist Berber dynasty with strong religious ideals. They expanded Marrakech and made significant architectural contributions that still define the city today.

The Almohads are perhaps best known for building the **Koutoubia Mosque**, one of the most recognizable landmarks in Marrakech, renowned for its towering minaret. During their reign, Marrakech saw the creation of large public spaces and infrastructure that promoted Islamic scholarship and culture.

The Almohads also made Marrakech a center for the arts, philosophy, and science. Their emphasis on intellectual and cultural development left a lasting legacy that helped shape the city's vibrant identity.

3. The Saadian Dynasty (1549–1659)

**The Golden Age of Marrakech**

After a period of decline, the Saadian dynasty restored Marrakech's former glory in the 16th century. Under Saadian rule, the city entered a golden age of prosperity and became the capital of Morocco once again. The dynasty's wealth, gained through trade, especially in sugar and gold, allowed them to finance stunning architectural projects.

One of the most famous contributions from this era is the **Saadian Tombs**, which reflect the Saadian flair for intricate decoration and luxurious design. The **El Badi Palace**, built by Sultan Ahmed al-Mansur, was a testament to the dynasty's power and wealth, though it now stands in ruins. The Saadians also invested in expanding the Medina, enhancing the city's infrastructure, and beautifying its gardens.

4. The Alaouite Dynasty (1666–Present)

**Restoration and Modernization**

The Alaouites, Morocco's current ruling dynasty, took control in the mid-17th century. While they shifted the capital to Fez and later to Rabat, Marrakech remained an important cultural and economic hub. Under Alaouite rule, Marrakech saw periods of both neglect and revival.

One of the key moments in modern Marrakech's history came in the late 19th century, when Sultan Moulay Hassan I rebuilt several parts of the city and restored key structures, ensuring Marrakech remained a key regional center. In the 20th century, as Morocco gained independence from France in 1956, Marrakech reemerged as a popular destination for travelers, artists, and adventurers from around the world.

5. The French Protectorate Period (1912–1956)

**Modernization Under Colonial Rule**

Although not a dynasty, the French Protectorate era had a lasting impact on Marrakech. During this period, the French introduced modern urban planning to the city, creating the new district of **Gueliz** outside the Medina, with wide streets and modern buildings. They also preserved many of the city's historic landmarks and contributed to its reputation as an exotic travel destination for Europeans.

Marrakech's infrastructure, including roads and services, was modernized, and the city began to attract international attention, with artists like Yves Saint Laurent and Winston Churchill visiting regularly. This fusion of colonial and traditional influences helped shape the city's modern identity.

Through the rise and fall of these dynasties, Marrakech has endured as a beacon of Moroccan history and culture. Each period brought its own developments, from the religious and architectural advancements of the

Almoravids and Almohads to the Saadian era's artistic flourish and the modernization efforts of the French. These layers of history make Marrakech a city where the past is ever-present, with each era adding to its unique character.

## Marrakech in Modern Times

Marrakech has gracefully evolved from its centuries-old roots into a city that seamlessly merges tradition with modernity. While the historic Medina still thrives as the heart of the city, packed with souks, palaces, and monuments, the rest of Marrakech has embraced the pace of contemporary life, becoming a bustling metropolis known for its culture, tourism, and innovation.

The Rise of Tourism

Marrakech has long attracted explorers, traders, and scholars, but in recent decades, it has become one of the most popular tourist destinations in the world. Since the 1960s, when figures like Yves Saint Laurent and The Beatles frequented the city, Marrakech has captured the imagination of artists, celebrities, and travelers alike. Its unique blend of traditional Moroccan culture, stunning architecture, and luxury tourism has cemented its reputation as a must-see destination.

Today, Marrakech's tourism industry thrives, with millions of visitors each year flocking to experience the city's rich history, food, and vibrant atmosphere. Medina, with its maze-like streets and colorful markets, remains a central draw, while modern districts like Gueliz and Hivernage offer upscale restaurants, boutiques, and hotels that cater to a more cosmopolitan crowd.

The Modern City: Gueliz and Hivernage

Beyond the ancient walls of the Medina lies the modern city, where Marrakech showcases its contemporary side. The district of **Gueliz**, developed during the French Protectorate, reflects European-style urban planning with wide streets, cafes, and trendy shops. This area has become a hub for shopping, dining, and modern living, offering an entirely different atmosphere from the bustling, labyrinthine Medina.

**Hivernage**, another modern neighborhood, is known for its luxury hotels, nightclubs, and upscale residential areas. These districts embody the city's shift toward modernity, attracting visitors who want to experience the best of both worlds—traditional Moroccan charm mixed with modern comforts.

Art, Fashion, and Culture

Marrakech's status as a global hub for art and culture has continued to grow, with the city now home to a vibrant contemporary art scene. Museums such as the **Marrakech Museum of Contemporary Art** and **Maison de la Photographie** showcase both traditional and modern Moroccan art, attracting artists from all over the world.

Fashion also plays a significant role in Marrakech's cultural identity. The city has hosted major international fashion events, and the legacy of **Yves Saint Laurent**, who made Marrakech his second home, continues to inspire. The **Yves Saint Laurent Museum**, located next to the famous **Majorelle Garden**, celebrates his iconic work and highlights the city's influence on his designs.

Preservation of Heritage

While embracing modernity, Marrakech has not lost sight of its deep cultural and architectural heritage. Efforts to preserve Medina and its historic landmarks remain strong, with organizations dedicated to maintaining the integrity of the city's ancient buildings. **UNESCO** declared the Medina of Marrakech a World Heritage site in 1985, ensuring that the city's rich history would be protected for future generations.

Additionally, there has been a growing emphasis on sustainable tourism, with efforts to preserve the natural beauty of Marrakech's gardens and promote eco-friendly practices in the city's hotels and riads. This balance between honoring the past and embracing the future is part of what makes modern-day Marrakech so dynamic.

A Global City

In recent years, Marrakech has positioned itself as a global city, drawing international businesses, conferences, and festivals. The city regularly hosts events such as the **Marrakech International Film Festival**, which brings world cinema to Morocco, and the **Marrakech Biennale**, a contemporary art festival that draws artists and visitors from across the globe.

Marrakech has also emerged as a center for tech and innovation in Morocco, with co-working spaces, tech hubs, and startups finding a foothold in the city. As Morocco invests in digital infrastructure, Marrakech is benefiting from the growth of its tech industry while remaining a place where tradition is deeply rooted in daily life.

Challenges and Opportunities

Like many cities experiencing rapid growth, Marrakech faces challenges in managing its modernization. As tourism continues to boom, there are concerns about overdevelopment and the strain on the city's infrastructure. Preserving the authenticity of the Medina and local communities, while accommodating the needs of modern visitors, is a delicate balance.

However, Marrakech's ability to blend the old and new is one of its greatest strengths. The city continues to find opportunities for growth while honoring its rich cultural heritage, ensuring it remains a unique destination where history and modernity coexist.

Looking Ahead

As Marrakech moves into the future, it remains a city of contrasts—a place where centuries-old traditions live alongside contemporary innovation. Its ability to evolve without losing its essence is what keeps Marrakech timeless, attracting visitors and residents who appreciate the city's past while embracing its future.

Whether you're exploring the ancient souks or dining in a trendy rooftop restaurant, Marrakech offers an experience that is truly one of a kind—a modern city grounded in a rich cultural legacy.

# Arriving in Marrakech

## Transportation: Flights and Getting Around

Marrakech is a well-connected city, making it easy to arrive and explore whether you're flying in from abroad or traveling from another part of Morocco. Once you land, there are several ways to navigate the city, from taxis and buses to exploring the winding streets of the Medina on foot.

Flying into Marrakech

Most international visitors arrive at **Marrakech Menara Airport (RAK)**, located about 6 kilometers (3.7 miles) from the city center. The airport serves major airlines from Europe, the Middle East, and Africa, with numerous direct flights from cities like Paris, London, Madrid, and Dubai.

**Arrival Process**:

Upon landing, you'll pass through immigration, where a valid passport is required for entry. Many nationalities do not need a visa for stays under 90 days, but it's worth checking the requirements in advance.

Once through customs, you'll find currency exchange counters and ATMs. It's a good idea to have some Moroccan dirhams (MAD) on hand before leaving the airport, as many small vendors and taxis prefer cash.

**Transportation Options from the Airport**:

**Taxi**: Taxis are readily available just outside the airport. Two types of taxis operate in Marrakech—**petit taxis** (small) for trips within the city and **grand taxis** for longer journeys, including trips to nearby cities or the airport. The fare to the city center from the airport typically ranges from 70 to 100 MAD, depending on your destination. It's best to agree on the fare before getting into the taxi, as many are not metered.

**Airport Shuttle**: The airport offers a shuttle bus (Line 19) that runs every 20-30 minutes from the terminal to central points like Jemaa el-Fnaa and the Gueliz district. The fare is affordable at around 30 MAD one way or 50 MAD for a round trip.

**Private Transfers**: Many hotels and riads offer private transfers from the airport. This is often the most comfortable and convenient option, especially if you're arriving late or with lots of luggage. It's wise to book this service ahead of time to avoid long waits.

Getting Around Marrakech

Once you've arrived in the city, navigating Marrakech depends largely on where you're staying and what you want to see. The ancient Medina, with its narrow, winding streets, is best explored on foot, while other parts of the city are easier to reach by car, taxi, or public transport.

**1. Walking**
The Medina is a pedestrian-friendly zone, where cars are often too big to navigate the tight streets. Walking is the best way to experience the heart of Marrakech, especially when exploring Jemaa el-Fnaa, the souks, and nearby attractions like the Koutoubia Mosque and Bahia Palace.

**Pro Tip**: Keep a map or navigation app handy, as the Medina's maze-like streets can be disorienting. Don't hesitate to ask locals for directions, but be aware that some may expect a small tip for helping.

**2. Taxis**
Taxis are the most common form of transportation in Marrakech, and you'll find plenty throughout the city.

**Petit Taxis**: These small, beige taxis are meant for travel within the city. They're usually metered, but it's common for drivers to negotiate a flat rate, especially in tourist areas. A typical ride within the city center costs around 20-30 MAD, but rates increase at night.

**Grand Taxis**: Larger and more comfortable than petit taxis, grand taxis are used for longer journeys, such as day trips to the Atlas Mountains or nearby cities. It's essential to agree on a price beforehand, as they typically don't use meters for long trips.

### 3. Buses

Marrakech has a public bus system that covers most areas of the city. Bus fares are extremely affordable, with a single ride costing around 4 MAD. While buses are efficient and cheap, they can be crowded and confusing for first-time visitors unfamiliar with the routes. However, if you're staying in the newer parts of the city like Gueliz or Hivernage, buses are a good option for getting around.

### 4. Car Rentals

If you plan to explore beyond Marrakech, such as a day trip to the Atlas Mountains or the Agafay Desert, renting a car is an option. There are several international and local car rental companies at the airport and throughout the city. However, driving within the city center is not recommended due to traffic congestion and the chaotic nature of the roads in the Medina. If you do rent a car, it's best used for excursions outside the city.

**Parking**: Parking in the Medina is scarce, but there are paid parking lots available outside the old city walls. Most hotels in modern areas have parking available.

## 5. Motorbikes and Bicycles

For a more adventurous way to get around, consider renting a motorbike or bicycle. This can be a fun way to explore Marrakech, especially for getting around the modern districts of Gueliz or Hivernage. However, Medina's crowded streets make biking or motorbiking a bit challenging for the unseasoned traveler.

## 6. Horse-Drawn Carriages (Calèches)

A popular and scenic way to explore Marrakech is by **calèche**, or horse-drawn carriage. These traditional carriages are often used for leisurely rides around the city, particularly in areas like the Koutoubia Mosque and the city's gardens. Prices should be negotiated before the ride, but a 30- to 60-minute ride typically costs between 150-250 MAD.

## 7. Private Drivers

For those looking for comfort and ease, hiring a private driver for the day is a great option. Many drivers double as informal guides and can take you to all the main sights, including excursions outside the city. Private drivers are especially useful for exploring areas like the Atlas Mountains, as they offer flexibility and local knowledge.

Navigating the Medina

Medina is a world of its own, and getting lost is almost part of the experience. While it's easy to lose your way in the labyrinth of narrow alleyways, this is often how you'll stumble upon hidden gems like tiny spice shops, local artisans, or lesser-known riads. That said, if you're in a hurry or feeling disoriented, locals are usually willing to guide you for a small tip.

**Pro Tip**: Be cautious when accepting help from strangers offering to lead you somewhere, as they may expect payment. It's best to ask shopkeepers or staff at your riad for directions or rely on offline maps on your phone.

## Understanding Local Customs and Etiquette

When visiting Marrakech, understanding local customs and etiquette can greatly enhance your experience and help you connect more meaningfully with the culture. Morocco is a predominantly Muslim country with deep-rooted traditions, and while the people of Marrakech are generally warm and welcoming to visitors, it's important to respect their cultural norms. Here are some key points to keep in mind during your stay.

1. Dress Code

Marrakech is a diverse city where you'll find locals dressed traditionally and tourists in more casual, Western clothing. However, it's important to be mindful of the conservative nature of Moroccan society, especially in more traditional areas like the Medina.

**For Women**: It's respectful to dress modestly, covering your shoulders, chest, and knees when walking around in public. Light, loose-fitting clothing is ideal to stay cool while still being respectful of local customs.

**For Men**: Men should also avoid wearing very short shorts or going shirtless. T-shirts and long pants or shorts that cover the knees are appropriate.

**In Tourist Areas**: In the modern parts of the city, like Gueliz or luxury resorts, the dress code is more relaxed, but it's still appreciated when visitors show modesty.

2. Greetings and Social Interactions

Moroccan people are known for their hospitality, and greetings are an important part of social etiquette.

**Greetings**: When meeting someone, a handshake is the most common greeting. Among close friends or family, men may greet each other with a kiss on both cheeks, starting with the left. However, it's best to follow the lead of the person you're meeting.

**For Women Travelers**: Handshakes between men and women can be more reserved. Some men may not initiate a handshake with a woman unless she offers her hand first. A polite "Salam" (hello) or nod is often sufficient if you're unsure.

**Use of Titles**: It's polite to address people with titles such as "Sidi" (Mr.) or "Lalla" (Mrs./Ms.) when speaking to them.

3. Visiting a Moroccan Home

If you're lucky enough to be invited into a Moroccan home, this is considered a great honor. Moroccan hospitality is legendary, and you will likely be treated to tea and snacks.

**Bringing Gifts**: It's customary to bring a small gift when visiting someone's home. Suitable options include sweets, pastries, or fresh fruit. Avoid bringing alcohol unless you know your host drinks it.

**Shoes**: You may be asked to remove your shoes before entering the home, especially in more traditional households. If in doubt, follow the lead of your host.

**Tea Ritual**: If offered tea, it's polite to accept, as tea is an important part of Moroccan hospitality. The host will often pour tea from a great height into small glasses, and it's customary to drink at least one glass, even if you don't want more.

4. Bargaining in the Souks

Bargaining is a common practice in Marrakech, especially in the souks (markets). It's not only expected but also part of the cultural experience.

**How to Bargain**: When buying goods in the souks, the initial price quoted by the vendor is usually inflated. It's expected that you will negotiate, and the final price often falls somewhere between half and two-thirds of the original asking price.

**Be Polite and Patient**: Bargaining is not just about getting the best deal—it's also a social interaction. Be patient, polite, and respectful during the process. Smiling and maintaining a friendly attitude will go a long way.

**When Not to Bargain**: Fixed prices are common in modern shops, restaurants, and some artisan cooperatives, where haggling is not appropriate.

5. Photography Etiquette

Marrakech is a photographer's dream, with its vibrant colors, intricate architecture, and bustling streets. However, it's important to be mindful when taking photos.

**Ask for Permission**: If you're photographing people, especially locals in the souks or public spaces, always ask for permission first. Some people may be uncomfortable being photographed, while others may expect a small tip in exchange for allowing you to take their picture.

**Religious Sites**: Be respectful when photographing mosques and religious sites. Non-Muslims are not permitted to enter many mosques in Morocco, and photography may be restricted in some areas.

6. Respect for Religion

Islam plays a central role in Moroccan culture, and there are several customs to be aware of to show respect for the local religion.

**Call to Prayer**: The call to prayer, known as the "adhan," is broadcast five times a day from mosques throughout the city. During this time, you may notice businesses slowing down and people heading to prayer. While you are not expected to participate, it's respectful to be mindful of this practice, especially when visiting religious sites or speaking with locals.

**Mosques**: Non-Muslims are generally not allowed to enter mosques in Marrakech, with the exception of the **Tin Mal Mosque**. However, you are welcome to admire the mosques from the outside and take photos from a distance.

**During Ramadan**: If visiting during the holy month of Ramadan, it's respectful to avoid eating, drinking, or smoking in public during daylight hours, as many locals will be fasting. Most restaurants and cafes in tourist areas will remain open, but it's courteous to be discreet.

7. Tipping

Tipping, or "baksheesh," is a common practice in Marrakech, and while it's not always obligatory, it's appreciated in many situations.

**Restaurants**: In restaurants, a tip of around 10% is customary, especially in more formal dining establishments. In smaller cafes, rounding up the bill is usually sufficient.

**Taxis and Guides**: It's customary to tip taxi drivers, guides, and hotel staff for their services. For taxi rides, rounding up to the nearest 5 or 10 MAD is appreciated, while for tour guides, tipping 50-100 MAD for a half-day or full-day tour is a standard practice.

**Street Performers**: In areas like Jemaa el-Fnaa, tipping street performers and musicians is expected if you stop to watch or take photos. A small tip of 5-10 MAD is appreciated.

8. Language

While Arabic is the official language of Morocco, the local dialect, Darija, is widely spoken. Berber is also spoken by many Moroccans, particularly in rural areas. French is commonly spoken in Marrakech, particularly in modern districts, restaurants, and hotels. Knowing a few basic phrases in Arabic or French will go a long way in showing respect to locals.

**Useful Phrases**:

"Salam Alaykum" – Peace be upon you (common greeting)

"Shukran" – Thank you

"La shukran" – No, thank you (polite refusal)

"Bslama" – Goodbye

## Essential Travel Tips for First-Time Visitors

Visiting Marrakech for the first time can be an exciting and enriching experience. The city's blend of vibrant culture, historical landmarks, and bustling markets makes it a fascinating destination, but it can also feel overwhelming if you're not prepared. These essential travel tips will help you navigate Marrakech smoothly and ensure that you make the most of your visit.

1. Currency and Money Exchange

The official currency of Morocco is the **Moroccan dirham (MAD)**. While credit cards are accepted in some hotels, restaurants, and larger stores, cash is still widely used, especially in the Medina and local markets.

**ATMs**: ATMs are plentiful in the city, especially in modern areas like Gueliz and Hivernage. It's a good idea to withdraw money in small amounts, as many places prefer exact change. Keep in mind that smaller shops and stalls in the souks may only accept cash.

**Currency Exchange**: You can exchange foreign currency at the airport, banks, or currency exchange bureaus throughout the city. Rates at the airport may be slightly higher, so consider exchanging only a small amount there and more at a bureau later. Be sure to keep receipts, as you'll need them if you want to exchange any unused dirhams back before leaving Morocco.

2. Language and Communication

While **Arabic** is the official language of Morocco, most people in Marrakech speak **Darija**, a Moroccan Arabic dialect. **French** is also widely spoken, particularly in modern areas and with businesses that cater to tourists.

**English**: In major tourist areas, you'll find many people who speak basic English, especially in hotels, restaurants, and souks. However, learning a few simple Arabic or French phrases will be greatly appreciated by locals and can enhance your experience.

**Basic Phrases**:

"Salam Alaykum" – Peace be upon you (hello)

"Shukran" – Thank you

"La shukran" – No, thank you

"Combien?" – How much? (French)

3. Best Time to Visit

Marrakech experiences a hot desert climate, with long, hot summers and mild winters. The best time to visit is typically in the **spring (March to May)** or **fall (September to November)**, when temperatures are more comfortable for exploring the city.

**Summer**: From June to August, temperatures can soar above 40°C (104°F), making it quite hot to explore during the day. If you visit during summer, plan outdoor activities early in the morning or late in the evening to avoid the heat.

**Winter**: Winters (December to February) are mild during the day but can be chilly at night, so bring layers if visiting during this time. Winter is also a quieter time for tourism, making it ideal for those who prefer fewer crowds.

4. Staying Safe

Marrakech is generally a safe city for travelers, but as with any destination, it's important to stay alert, particularly in crowded areas like the Medina and Jemaa el-Fnaa.

**Pickpocketing**: Keep an eye on your belongings, especially in busy markets. Use a crossbody bag that can be zipped and avoid carrying large amounts of cash. Be cautious of people offering unsolicited help or services, as they may expect a tip in return.

**Getting Lost in the Medina**: The Medina's narrow streets can be confusing, so it's easy to get lost. Carry a map or use an offline navigation app. If you need help, it's better to ask a shopkeeper or a local business owner for directions rather than strangers on the street.

**Scams**: Be cautious of common tourist scams, such as being offered "free" henna tattoos or being told that a particular attraction is closed so that you'll be redirected to a different (and more expensive) location. Politely decline and verify any claims with official sources.

5. Drinking Water

While bottled water is widely available in Marrakech and recommended for drinking, most locals drink tap water. However, to avoid any stomach issues, it's best for tourists to stick to bottled water for drinking, brushing teeth, and washing fruits or vegetables.

**Bottled Water**: You can buy bottled water at most convenience stores, supermarkets, and cafes. Look for sealed bottles to ensure the water is safe to drink.

**Ice**: It's also advisable to avoid ice in drinks, especially from street vendors, as it may be made from tap water.

6. Local Cuisine and Dining

Marrakech is a food lover's paradise, offering a mix of rich Moroccan dishes that are both flavorful and fragrant. Trying local food is a must, but there are a few things to keep in mind.

**Street Food**: Street food in Jemaa el-Fnaa is popular and usually safe to eat, but stick to stalls with a high turnover of food to ensure freshness. Moroccan dishes such as **tagine**, **couscous**, and **pastilla** are local specialties you won't want to miss.

**Vegetarian/Vegan Options**: While many Moroccan dishes are meat-based, vegetarian options are widely available. You can find vegetable tagines, salads, and couscous dishes, and most restaurants will accommodate dietary preferences if you ask.

**Tipping**: Tipping is common in restaurants and cafes, with a typical tip of around 10% of the bill.

7. Transportation Tips

Navigating Marrakech is relatively easy once you understand the available transportation options.

**Taxis**: **Petit taxis** are small, metered taxis that operate within the city. Always ensure the meter is running, or negotiate a price before starting your ride. **Grand taxis** are larger and typically used for longer journeys outside the city. If you're unsure of the fare, ask your hotel or locals for guidance.

**Walking**: The best way to explore the Medina is on foot, but be prepared for the narrow and often crowded streets. Comfortable shoes are essential for navigating the city's cobbled paths.

**Buses**: Marrakech has an affordable public bus system, but it may be confusing for first-time visitors. Stick to taxis or walking if you're unsure of bus routes.

## 8. Shopping in the Souks

Marrakech's souks are a major attraction, offering a colorful array of handcrafted goods, spices, carpets, and pottery. Bargaining is expected, and it's part of the shopping experience.

**Bargaining**: Always negotiate the price, but do so politely. Start by offering about half the initial price quoted and work your way to a fair compromise. Remember that bargaining is a friendly exchange, and it's important to stay respectful.

**Avoiding Fake Goods**: Be cautious when buying luxury brand items in the souks, as many are counterfeit. Focus instead on authentic Moroccan goods like **handmade carpets**, **leather goods**, **lanterns**, and **spices**.

## 9. Respect Local Customs

Marrakech is a predominantly Muslim city, and it's important to respect local customs and traditions.

**Modest Dress**: While tourists are not required to follow local dress codes strictly, dressing modestly (covering shoulders and knees) is appreciated, especially when visiting religious sites.

**Photography**: Always ask for permission before taking photos of people, especially in the Medina. Some locals may request a small tip in exchange for being photographed.

**Religious Sites**: Non-Muslims are not allowed to enter most mosques, including the Koutoubia Mosque, but you can admire the beautiful architecture from the outside.

10. Staying Connected

Wi-Fi is widely available in Marrakech, especially in hotels, riads, and cafes. However, if you need constant access to the internet or navigation apps, consider buying a local SIM card.

**Local SIM Cards**: SIM cards are inexpensive and available at the airport or in telecom shops throughout the city. The major providers are **Maroc Telecom**, **Orange**, and **Inwi**, and they offer affordable data plans for tourists.

# Exploring the Medina

## Jemaa el-Fnaa: The Heart of Marrakech

At the center of Marrakech's historic Medina lies **Jemaa el-Fnaa**, one of the most famous and lively public squares in the world. This bustling marketplace and cultural hub is the beating heart of the city, drawing locals and tourists alike to its vibrant atmosphere. By day, it is a lively market square, but by night, it transforms into an open-air theater filled with entertainers, food vendors, and the aromas of Moroccan cuisine. Jemaa el-Fnaa is truly the pulse of Marrakech, and no visit to the city is complete without experiencing its unique energy.

A Living Stage of Culture and Entertainment

Jemaa el-Fnaa has been a gathering place for centuries and is a UNESCO World Heritage site, recognized for its role in preserving Morocco's living traditions. The square is a kaleidoscope of sounds, sights, and smells, with a variety of performances and activities taking place throughout the day.

**Daytime Scene**: During the day, Jemaa el-Fnaa serves as a marketplace and cultural space. You'll find snake charmers swaying to the rhythm of their flutes, henna artists offering intricate designs, and stalls selling fresh orange juice, dates, and nuts. Storytellers and musicians often gather small crowds, passing down ancient Moroccan tales and tunes.

**Nighttime Transformation**: As the sun sets, Jemaa el-Fnaa transforms into an entirely different experience. Rows of food stalls emerge, filling the air with the smell of grilled meats, tagines, and spiced couscous. Performers, including traditional dancers, acrobats, and Gnawa musicians, fill the square, creating a festival-like atmosphere. Lanterns and lights glow, making the square feel magical and otherworldly.

**Street Performers**: Whether you're watching Berber drummers, acrobatic shows, or the mysterious movements of snake charmers, the performers in Jemaa el-Fnaa add to its allure. Each performance feels spontaneous, and the variety of acts showcases the cultural diversity of Morocco.

Food Stalls and Moroccan Delicacies

One of the highlights of Jemaa el-Fnaa is the incredible range of food stalls that pop up in the evening, offering an authentic taste of Moroccan cuisine at affordable prices. These temporary restaurants serve everything from grilled kebabs and lamb to vegetable tagines and fresh salads.

**What to Try**:

**Grilled Meats**: Skewers of marinated chicken, beef, and lamb are grilled to perfection and served with bread, olives, and spicy dipping sauces.

**Tagine**: Morocco's signature slow-cooked dish is made with meat or vegetables, stewed in a clay pot with rich spices like saffron, cumin, and cinnamon.

**Harira**: A traditional Moroccan soup made from lentils, tomatoes, and chickpeas, often eaten as a starter.

**Snails**: For the adventurous eater, try a bowl of snails cooked in a fragrant broth spiced with cumin and other local spices.

**Fresh Juices**: During the day, you'll find stalls selling freshly squeezed orange juice for a refreshing treat. At night, try Moroccan tea or fruit smoothies.

**Tips for Eating at Jemaa el-Fnaa**:

Choose stalls with a lot of local customers, as this is often a sign of good quality and hygiene.

Don't be afraid to ask the vendors about the dishes before ordering—most are happy to explain their offerings.

Prices can vary, so it's a good idea to ask for the price of a meal before sitting down.

Shopping in and Around the Square

While Jemaa el-Fnaa itself isn't primarily a shopping destination, it serves as a gateway to the nearby souks, where you can shop for a wide variety of traditional Moroccan goods.

**The Souks**: Behind the square lies a maze of interconnected alleys filled with souks (markets) selling everything from spices and carpets to leather goods and lanterns. The souks are organized by craft, so you'll find entire sections dedicated to specific items like metalwork, textiles, and jewelry. It's an excellent place to practice your bargaining skills, and many of the goods on offer are handmade by skilled artisans.

**What to Buy**:

**Spices**: The spice shops near Jemaa el-Fnaa are brimming with colorful piles of cumin, saffron, cinnamon, and the famous Moroccan spice mix, **ras el hanout**.

**Handmade Carpets**: The souks offer beautiful handwoven carpets, each one telling its own story through unique patterns and colors.

**Leather Goods**: Marrakech is known for its high-quality leather, and you can find everything from bags and shoes to belts and wallets.

**Argan Oil**: Morocco's famous argan oil, known for its cosmetic and culinary uses, is a popular item to purchase as a souvenir.

A Hub for Storytelling

One of the unique aspects of Jemaa el-Fnaa is its role in preserving Morocco's oral storytelling tradition. Storytellers, or **halqa**, have gathered in the square for centuries, sharing folktales, historical events, and lessons through engaging narratives. Although this tradition has declined in recent years, it's still possible to catch a storyteller captivating a crowd, particularly in the evenings.

**Language Barrier**: The stories are often told in Arabic or Berber, but even if you don't understand the language, watching the storyteller's animated performance and the crowd's reactions is an experience in itself.

Safety and Tips for Visitors

While Jemaa el-Fnaa is a safe place to explore, it's important to be mindful of your surroundings, especially as the square can become very crowded in the evenings.

**Pickpocketing**: As with any busy area, keep your valuables secure and be aware of pickpockets. A crossbody bag with zippers is a good option to keep your belongings safe.

**Street Performers**: If you watch a performance or take photos of street performers, it's customary to leave a small tip, as this is often how the performers make a living. Keep small denominations of dirhams (5-10 MAD) handy for this purpose.

**Henna Artists**: While some henna artists are reputable, others may attempt to apply henna without your consent and then demand payment. Politely decline if you don't wish to have henna applied.

### The Soul of Marrakech

Jemaa el-Fnaa is more than just a square; it's a reflection of Marrakech's vibrant soul. It's a place where the past and present meet, where ancient traditions like storytelling and snake charming coexist with modern street food and bustling crowds. For many, it's the gateway to discovering the heart of the city—a place of endless fascination and energy.

Whether you're sipping fresh orange juice while watching the world go by, wandering through the stalls at night, or simply soaking in the atmosphere, Jemaa el-Fnaa offers an unforgettable experience that captures the spirit of Marrakech.

## Navigating the Souks Shopping for Spices, Textiles, and Crafts

The souks of Marrakech are a sensory experience like no other, offering a treasure trove of handcrafted goods, fragrant spices, and stunning textiles. Tucked behind the bustling square of Jemaa el-Fnaa, the souks are a labyrinth of narrow alleyways filled with shops and stalls, each specializing in different products. Whether you're searching for aromatic spices, vibrant carpets, or intricate ceramics, navigating the souks is an adventure in itself. With the right approach, you can discover beautiful keepsakes and bargains while immersing yourself in the culture of Marrakech.

Understanding the Souks

The souks are divided into distinct areas, each dedicated to a specific type of good, making it easier to find what you're looking for. However, be prepared to get lost in the maze of winding streets—this is part of the charm, and often leads to unexpected discoveries.

**Souk Semmarine**: One of the main arteries of the souks, leading from Jemaa el-Fnaa, Souk Semmarine is home to a wide range of items, including textiles, shoes, and traditional Moroccan clothing. This is a good starting point for your shopping journey.

**Souk el Kebir**: Known for its leather goods, this area of the souks is where you'll find bags, belts, shoes, and wallets made from high-quality Moroccan leather.

**Rahba Kedima Square**: This square is famous for its spice markets, and the scent of cumin, saffron, and cinnamon fills the air. It's also a great place to buy baskets and other handcrafted goods.

**Souk des Teinturiers**: Also known as the Dyer's Souk, this area is where you'll find vivid textiles and yarns hanging out to dry. The colorful displays are a photographer's dream, and it's a great spot for purchasing scarves, fabrics, and traditional Berber clothing.

Shopping for Spices

The spice stalls in the souks are not only a feast for the senses but also a window into Morocco's rich culinary traditions. You'll see piles of colorful spices—yellow turmeric, red paprika, green mint leaves—each with its own unique fragrance and flavor.

**Spices to Buy**:

**Ras el Hanout**: A blend of 20 or more spices, this versatile mix is used in many Moroccan dishes like tagines and couscous. Each vendor has their own version of ras el hanout, so it's worth sampling a few before buying.

**Saffron**: One of the most valuable spices, Moroccan saffron is prized for its delicate flavor and vibrant color. Make sure you're buying genuine saffron, as some vendors may try to pass off lower-quality substitutes.

**Cumin and Cinnamon**: Two staples of Moroccan cooking, cumin is used to add depth to savory dishes, while cinnamon is often added to tagines and desserts for a warm, sweet flavor.

**Argan Oil**: While not a spice, argan oil is a Moroccan specialty often used in cooking. The culinary version of this oil is rich in flavor and packed with nutrients.

**How to Buy Spices**:

Spices are typically sold by weight, so you can buy as much or as little as you need. Don't hesitate to ask the vendor for a sample or to explain how a spice is used in Moroccan cooking.

Bargaining is expected, but remember to keep it friendly. Start by offering half of the quoted price and work your way to a fair agreement.

Shopping for Textiles

Marrakech is a paradise for textile lovers. From hand woven Berber carpets to colorful scarves and kaftans, the souks offer a wide array of fabrics and clothing that reflect Morocco's diverse cultural influences.

**Berber Carpets**: The souks are famous for their hand woven Berber carpets, each one telling a story through its intricate patterns and vibrant colors. You'll find both **Beni Ourain** rugs, known for their simple geometric designs and neutral colors, and **kilim** rugs, which feature bold colors and tribal motifs. Buying a carpet is a more significant investment, so take your time to inspect the quality, ask about its origin, and be prepared to negotiate the price.

**Scarves and Shawls**: The Dyer's Souk is the place to find brightly colored scarves, pashminas, and shawls made from silk, wool, or cotton. These make for beautiful and practical souvenirs that can also protect you from the sun while exploring the Medina.

**Traditional Clothing**: If you're looking for a kaftan or djellaba (traditional Moroccan robes), Souk Semmarine offers a range of options. These garments are often embellished with intricate embroidery and make for great gifts or personal keepsakes.

**Tips for Buying Textiles**:

**Inspect the Fabric**: Check the quality of the fabric before buying. Handwoven textiles often have slight imperfections, which add to their charm, but ensure the overall quality is good.

**Bargain Politely**: As with most purchases in the souks, bargaining is expected. However, don't feel pressured to buy immediately. Take your time, compare prices, and always remain respectful during negotiations.

Shopping for Crafts

The souks are filled with artisans creating traditional Moroccan crafts, from pottery to lanterns and leather goods. These handmade items make wonderful souvenirs and reflect the craftsmanship that has been passed down through generations.

- **Ceramics**: You'll find beautiful ceramics in a range of colors and designs, from **tagine pots** to intricately painted bowls and plates. The best ceramics often come from the town of Safi, but you'll find a great selection in the Marrakech souks as well.

**Lanterns**: Moroccan lanterns, with their delicate metalwork and intricate designs, are one of the most iconic souvenirs you can buy. Whether you're looking for a large hanging lantern or a smaller tabletop piece, these make for stunning décor items.

**Leather Goods**: Moroccan leather is famous for its quality, and the souks offer a range of leather products, from handbags and belts to wallets and poufs. The leather goods are often handmade and dyed using traditional methods in the city's tanneries.

**How to Buy Crafts**:

**Check Craftsmanship**: When buying pottery or leather goods, examine the craftsmanship to ensure you're purchasing high-quality items. For example, a well-made lantern will have clean, intricate metalwork with no rough edges.

**Ask About the Process**: Many artisans are proud to explain the process behind their craft. Take the opportunity to ask questions about the materials and techniques used, as this can give you a greater appreciation of the item you're buying.

Bargaining: The Art of Negotiation

Bargaining is part of the shopping experience in Marrakech, and it's expected in almost every transaction. While the idea of haggling may seem daunting at first, it's a friendly and enjoyable process once you get the hang of it. The key is to remain polite, patient, and flexible.

**How to Bargain**:

Start by offering about half of the vendor's initial price and be prepared to go back and forth. The goal is to reach a price that both you and the vendor are happy with.

Don't rush the process—bargaining is often accompanied by friendly conversation. It's common for vendors to offer you tea as part of the interaction, especially if you're purchasing a higher-value item like a carpet or lantern.

If you feel the price is too high or you're not interested, don't be afraid to walk away. Often, the vendor will call you back with a lower offer.

**Cultural Considerations**:

Bargaining is seen as part of Moroccan culture, so approach it with a positive attitude. It's not about "winning" the negotiation but rather finding a fair price through friendly discussion.

Always maintain respect and avoid aggressive tactics. If a vendor seems unwilling to lower the price significantly, it may be because the item is of higher quality or has more sentimental value.

Final Tips for Shopping in the Souks

**Take Your Time**: The souks can be overwhelming, so give yourself plenty of time to explore, wander, and appreciate the artistry around you.

**Carry Cash**: Many vendors do not accept credit cards, so it's essential to have cash on hand. Be sure to carry small bills, as change can be hard to come by.

**Pack Light**: Leave some room in your luggage for the treasures you'll want to take home. If you plan to buy larger items like carpets or lanterns, many vendors offer international shipping.

The souks of Marrakech are more than just a shopping destination—they're a window into Morocco's rich cultural heritage. By navigating the markets with an open mind and a sense of adventure, you'll come away with not only unique treasures but also memories of an authentic Moroccan experience.

## Key Landmarks Koutoubia Mosque, Ben Youssef Madrasa, and Saadian Tombs

Marrakech is home to some of Morocco's most stunning architectural and historical landmarks, each offering a glimpse into the city's rich cultural and religious heritage. Among the most notable are the **Koutoubia Mosque**, the **Ben Youssef Madrasa**, and the **Saadian Tombs**. These sites not only showcase the artistry of Moroccan architecture but also provide insight into the city's Islamic and dynastic history. Whether you're interested in history, religion, or design, these landmarks are must-see stops on your journey through Marrakech.

Koutoubia Mosque

### The Iconic Symbol of Marrakech

The **Koutoubia Mosque**, also known as the **Mosque of the Booksellers**, is the largest mosque in Marrakech and one of the most iconic landmarks in the city. Towering over the Medina, the mosque's **77-meter (253 feet)** minaret dominates the skyline and serves as a point of orientation for those wandering the winding streets of the old city. The mosque is named after the "kutubiyyin," or booksellers, who once had their bookstalls in the area surrounding the mosque.

**History**: Built in the 12th century during the reign of the Almohad Caliph Yaqub al-Mansur, the Koutoubia Mosque is considered a masterpiece of Almohad architecture. Its towering minaret, adorned with intricate geometric designs and topped with copper orbs, has influenced other significant mosques, including the Giralda in Seville and the Hassan Tower in Rabat.

**Architecture**: The mosque features traditional Moroccan architectural elements, including **horseshoe arches**, decorative tiles, and carved stucco detailing. The minaret, designed with four copper orbs, is the crowning feature of the mosque, making it a visual landmark throughout the city. The structure is built with red sandstone, in keeping with the "red city" aesthetic of Marrakech.

**Visiting Tips**:

Non-Muslims are not allowed to enter the mosque, but you can admire the building and its minaret from outside, as well as enjoy the surrounding **Koutoubia Gardens**, which offer a peaceful place to relax and take in the view.

The call to prayer from the Koutoubia Mosque fills the air five times a day, a reminder of the city's deep Islamic roots.

Ben Youssef Madrasa

**A Masterpiece of Islamic Learning and Architecture**

The **Ben Youssef Madrasa** is one of the most beautiful and historically significant landmarks in Marrakech. This Islamic college was once the largest in Morocco, where students came to study the Quran and Islamic law. Today, the madrasa stands as a testament to Morocco's rich intellectual and artistic traditions.

**History**: The madrasa was founded in the 14th century by the Merenid Sultan Abu al-Hasan and later rebuilt by the Saadian Sultan Abdallah al-Ghalib in the 16th century. It operated as a center for Islamic learning for over 400 years until it was closed in 1960. After undergoing restoration, the madrasa was opened to the public as a historical site in 1982.

**Architecture**: The Ben Youssef Madrasa is renowned for its stunning Moorish design, featuring a large courtyard adorned with **zellige tiles**, **carved cedar wood**, and **stucco detailing**. The madrasa's **prayer hall** is equally impressive, with its elaborate mihrab and high domed ceiling. The madrasa also has a dormitory where students once lived, with 132 small, plain rooms surrounding the courtyard.

The central courtyard is the heart of the madrasa, with a reflective pool at its center and a blend of **geometric patterns** and **Arabic calligraphy** decorating the walls. The intricate craftsmanship of the plaster and wood carvings is breathtaking, offering visitors a glimpse of the height of Islamic art and architecture.

**Visiting Tips**:

The madrasa is open to visitors, and you can freely explore the dormitories, prayer hall, and stunning courtyard.

Take your time to appreciate the intricate tilework and carvings that reflect the height of Saadian craftsmanship.

Photography is allowed, and the madrasa is a favorite spot for capturing the beauty of Moroccan architecture up close.

Saadian Tombs

**Resting Place of Royalty and Artistic Masterpiece**

The **Saadian Tombs** are one of Marrakech's most significant historical sites, dating back to the time of the Saadian dynasty in the 16th century. The tombs are the final resting place of Sultan Ahmed al-Mansur and his family, as well as many other members of the Saadian dynasty, who ruled over Morocco during one of its most prosperous periods.

**History**: The tombs were built during the reign of Sultan Ahmed al-Mansur in the late 1500s, and they were used as a burial ground for the Saadian royal family. After the fall of the dynasty, the tombs were sealed and fell into obscurity for centuries until they were rediscovered in 1917. The tombs have since been restored and are now one of the most visited sites in Marrakech.

**Architecture**: The Saadian Tombs are known for their stunning decoration, reflecting the opulence of the Saadian era. The tombs are housed in two main mausoleums, featuring **Italian Carrara marble**, **intricate tilework**, and lavish plaster carvings. The highlight of the tombs is the **Hall of the Twelve Columns**, where Sultan Ahmed al-Mansur is buried. The hall is adorned with beautifully carved cedar wood, zellige tiles, and stucco, making it one of the finest examples of Saadian craftsmanship.

The site also includes a garden filled with palm trees and other greenery, creating a peaceful atmosphere around the tombs.

**Visiting Tips**:

The Saadian Tombs are located near the **Kasbah Mosque** in the southern part of the Medina. The site can get crowded, especially during peak tourist seasons, so visiting early in the morning is recommended.

Take time to explore the different mausoleums and admire the intricate details in the marble and stucco work. The craftsmanship of the Saadian period is some of the finest in Morocco.

Don't miss the beautiful **gardens** surrounding the tombs, where you can take a quiet moment to reflect on the history of the Saadian dynasty.

The Koutoubia Mosque, Ben Youssef Madrasa, and Saadian Tombs are more than just architectural marvels—they are a testament to the rich history and cultural heritage of Marrakech. Each of these landmarks offers visitors a deeper understanding of the city's religious, educational, and dynastic past, making them essential stops on any trip to Marrakech.

Whether you're gazing up at the towering minaret of the Koutoubia Mosque, exploring the intricate tilework of the Ben Youssef Madrasa, or walking through the ornate mausoleums of the Saadian Tombs, these landmarks capture the essence of Marrakech's beauty and history.

# Marrakech's Architectural Wonders

## Bahia Palace: A Glimpse into Moroccan Royalty

The **Bahia Palace**, a stunning example of Moroccan architecture, offers visitors a window into the opulent world of 19th-century Moroccan royalty. Nestled in the southern part of Marrakech's Medina, the palace is a masterpiece of intricate design, blending traditional Moroccan craftsmanship with Andalusian influence. "Bahia," meaning "brilliance," perfectly describes the dazzling courtyards, lush gardens, and ornate interiors that once served as the home of Morocco's ruling elite.

History of Bahia Palace

Construction of the Bahia Palace began in the 1860s under the orders of **Si Moussa**, the grand vizier of Sultan Hassan I, as a private residence. It was expanded in the 1890s by **Ba Ahmed**, Si Moussa's son, who also served as vizier and regent. Ba Ahmed envisioned a palace that would reflect the power and wealth of the royal court, sparing no expense in its construction. While the palace was never completed, what remains today is a testament to Morocco's architectural brilliance during the Saadian and Alaouite dynasties.

Ba Ahmed used the palace as his official residence, housing his wives, concubines, and extended family, while also hosting foreign dignitaries and conducting state affairs. After his death in 1900, the palace was looted, but its structural beauty has survived, making it one of Marrakech's most admired historical landmarks.

Architecture and Design

Bahia Palace is a striking example of Moroccan and Moorish architecture, characterized by the use of **zellige tiles**, **carved cedar wood**, and **stucco ornamentation**. Covering over 8 hectares, the palace consists of lavish courtyards, interconnected rooms, and stunning gardens, all designed to create an atmosphere of luxury and serenity.

**Courtyards and Gardens**: The palace's layout revolves around open courtyards, the largest of which is the **Grand Courtyard**, an expansive space paved with Italian **Carrara marble**. Surrounding the courtyards are lush gardens filled with **orange trees**, **fountains**, and greenery that provide a tranquil setting amid the palace's grandeur.

**Zellige Tilework**: Bahia Palace's walls and floors are adorned with **zellige**—a form of glazed terracotta tilework arranged in intricate geometric patterns. The vibrant colors and designs showcase the artistry of

Moroccan craftsmen, creating a kaleidoscope of shapes that reflect the palace's luxurious atmosphere.

**Wooden Ceilings**: One of the most remarkable features of the palace is its **cedar wood ceilings**, intricately carved and painted with geometric and floral motifs. These ceilings are a highlight in rooms like the **Salon of Honor**, where guests would have been entertained in surroundings meant to impress.

**Stucco and Arabesques**: Delicate plasterwork known as **stucco** decorates the palace walls, with intricate **arabesques** and floral patterns. These elements, combined with carved cedar and tilework, represent the pinnacle of Moroccan craftsmanship during the palace's construction.

Exploring the Bahia Palace

Visitors are free to explore many areas of Bahia Palace, each offering a unique look at the opulence of 19th-century Moroccan royalty. Some of the most captivating sections include:

**The Grand Courtyard**: The centerpiece of Bahia Palace, this open space is lined with marble floors and surrounded by ornately decorated rooms. The symmetrical design of the courtyard creates a peaceful atmosphere, enhanced by the orange trees and fountains.

**The Harem Quarters**: Ba Ahmed's wives and concubines lived in the more secluded quarters of the palace, which feature smaller rooms but equally lavish details. The harem area offers insight into the private lives of Moroccan royalty, with rooms that open onto intimate courtyards.

**The Reception Rooms**: These large, formal rooms were used to host important guests and diplomatic meetings. The intricately carved wooden ceilings and tilework in these spaces reflect the grandeur and sophistication intended to leave an impression on visitors.

Visiting Tips

**Best Time to Visit**: Bahia Palace can get crowded, particularly during peak tourist seasons. To enjoy a quieter experience, visit early in the morning or later in the afternoon. The palace is open daily from 9 AM to 5 PM.

**What to Look For**: Take time to appreciate the details in the tilework, ceilings, and courtyards. Each section of the palace tells a story, so wander slowly and allow yourself to absorb the intricate artistry.

**Photography**: Bahia Palace is a photographer's dream, with its play of light and shadow, vibrant tiles, and beautiful gardens. Photography is allowed, so bring your camera to capture the stunning details of this architectural wonder.

**Guided Tours**: To gain a deeper understanding of the palace's history and design, consider hiring a guide. Many guides are available at the entrance, or you can arrange for a private tour ahead of time.

The Legacy of Bahia Palace

Bahia Palace stands as a symbol of Morocco's architectural and cultural heritage. Though its grandeur was built to reflect the power of Morocco's ruling elite, today, it serves as a historical landmark that continues to awe visitors with its beauty. The palace's design—rich with geometric precision, artistic flair, and harmonious balance—reflects the height of Moroccan craftsmanship during the 19th century.

The palace offers more than just a glimpse into the past; it is a living representation of the cultural synthesis that defined Morocco's art and architecture. Whether you're admiring the ornate ceilings, wandering through the peaceful courtyards, or contemplating the intricacies of the tilework, Bahia Palace is a place where history, art, and royalty converge.

## El Badi Palace Ruins of a Majestic Past

Once the epitome of luxury and grandeur, the **El Badi Palace** in Marrakech now stands in majestic ruins, a haunting reminder of Morocco's opulent Saadian dynasty. Built in the late 16th century by Sultan Ahmed al-Mansur to celebrate his victory over the Portuguese at the Battle of the Three Kings, the palace was a symbol of wealth, power, and royal prestige. Though it was later stripped of its treasures, El Badi Palace remains an iconic site that transports visitors back to a time of royal extravagance and architectural splendor.

History of El Badi Palace

Construction of El Badi Palace began in 1578, funded by the immense wealth Sultan Ahmed al-Mansur gained from his military victories and from trade, particularly in gold and sugar. The palace, whose name means "The Incomparable," was intended to showcase the grandeur of the Saadian dynasty and solidify Ahmed al-Mansur's legacy.

The palace took over 25 years to complete, with artisans from across Morocco, Spain, and Italy contributing to its elaborate design. It was adorned with the finest materials, including **Italian marble**, **gold leaf**, and intricate tilework. At the height of its glory, El Badi Palace had 360 rooms, grand pavilions, sunken gardens, and expansive courtyards. The central courtyard was particularly impressive, featuring a vast pool surrounded by orange trees and fountains.

Despite its splendor, El Badi Palace had a brief reign of grandeur. In the 17th century, the Alaouite Sultan Moulay Ismail, determined to erase the legacy of the Saadian rulers, ordered the palace to be dismantled. The precious materials were stripped and used to construct his own palace in Meknes, leaving El Badi a shadow of its former self. Today, only the walls and foundations of the once-grand palace remain, but even in ruins, the site offers a glimpse of its former majesty.

Architecture and Layout

Though El Badi Palace is now largely in ruins, its layout and architectural design are still visible and provide insight into the opulence of its past.

**The Central Courtyard**: The centerpiece of El Badi Palace is its massive **courtyard**, one of the largest in Morocco. Measuring about 135 meters by 110 meters, the courtyard is dominated by a large rectangular pool, which would have reflected the grand pavilions that once stood around it. The courtyard's symmetry and open space create an overwhelming sense of scale, giving visitors a feel for the sheer size of the palace.

**The Pavilions**: Four grand pavilions originally surrounded the courtyard, each showcasing intricate **zellige tilework**, **carved cedar ceilings**, and rich stucco decoration. Although the pavilions no longer stand in their original form, their foundations and a few remaining walls hint at the luxury they once embodied.

**Sunken Gardens**: Surrounding the pool were lush **sunken gardens**, planted with orange trees and other vegetation. These gardens provided a peaceful contrast to the grandeur of the palace's architecture and were designed to create a serene, natural atmosphere amid the luxury.

**Underground Tunnels and Dungeons**: Beneath the palace lie **underground tunnels** and **dungeons**, which visitors can still explore today. These were likely used as storage areas or possibly as prison cells, adding a mysterious and darker element to the palace's history.

Exploring El Badi Palace

While much of El Badi Palace has been reduced to ruins, visitors can still explore the vast site, which offers an impressive view of the original layout and scale of the palace. The crumbling walls, towering over the sunlit courtyards, create a dramatic atmosphere that makes the ruins feel alive with history.

**The Minbar of the Koutoubia Mosque**: One of the palace's most famous attractions today is the restored **Minbar of the Koutoubia Mosque**, a 12th-century pulpit that was crafted in Cordoba, Spain, and later brought to Marrakech. This intricately carved and decorated wooden pulpit is displayed in a museum space within the palace and is considered one of the finest examples of Islamic woodwork in the world.

**Panoramic Views**: Climbing to the top of the remaining walls offers panoramic views of the **Medina**, the **Atlas Mountains**, and the surrounding cityscape. This vantage point gives visitors a sense of the palace's strategic location and the impressive scale it once commanded.

**Storks' Nests**: Today, the palace is also home to large **storks' nests**, adding a unique element to the ruins. These birds have made the towering walls of El Badi their home, and their nests add a natural element to the once-magnificent palace, making the site feel alive in a new way.

Visiting Tips

**Best Time to Visit**: The palace can get hot in the summer, so it's best to visit early in the morning or later in the afternoon. The open courtyards provide little shade, so bring a hat and sunscreen.

**What to Explore**: Take time to explore the remaining walls and foundations, as well as the underground dungeons and storage areas, which offer a sense of the palace's former grandeur. Don't miss the Minbar exhibit for a closer look at a masterpiece of Islamic art.

**Photography**: The stark beauty of the ruins, combined with the light and shadows cast across the open courtyards, makes El Badi Palace a photographer's dream. The panoramic views from the walls provide a stunning backdrop for photographs of the surrounding city.

The Legacy of El Badi Palace

Although El Badi Palace stands in ruins, its legacy as a symbol of Morocco's rich history and architectural brilliance remains intact. Once a dazzling showcase of Saadian wealth and power, the palace now serves as a testament to the transience of royal grandeur. The ruins offer visitors a poignant reminder of the Saadian dynasty's rise and fall, while the scale and layout of the site still impress, even centuries after its heyday.

El Badi Palace may no longer shine with the gold and marble that once adorned its walls, but its architectural footprint and the stories it holds continue to captivate visitors from around the world. Exploring the ruins of this majestic palace is a journey through a fascinating chapter of Marrakech's royal history, where even in decay, the grandeur of the past can still be felt.

## The Majestic Riads of Marrakech

Hidden behind the bustling streets of Marrakech's Medina are some of the city's most enchanting treasures: the **riads**. These traditional Moroccan houses, characterized by their inward-facing design and serene courtyards, offer a peaceful escape from the lively atmosphere outside. Often converted into boutique hotels or guesthouses, the riads of Marrakech are known for their architectural beauty, intricate craftsmanship, and intimate ambiance. For many visitors, staying in a riad is one of the most memorable experiences in Marrakech, offering a perfect blend of Moroccan history, culture, and hospitality.

What is a Riad?

The word "riad" comes from the Arabic term for **garden**—and appropriately so, as the focal point of any riad is its courtyard, often filled with lush greenery, fountains, and tiled walkways. Riads are typically designed around this central courtyard, with all rooms and windows facing inward, offering privacy and tranquility. This design, common in traditional Moroccan homes, is meant to provide an oasis of calm, insulating the inhabitants from the heat, noise, and activity of the city.

The inward-facing layout also reflects Moroccan cultural values, particularly the importance of family life and the need for privacy within the home. This creates a strong contrast with the often chaotic and vibrant streets of the Medina outside.

Architecture and Design

Riads are a showcase of Moroccan craftsmanship, featuring traditional design elements that reflect the city's rich cultural heritage. Many of Marrakech's riads date back centuries, and though they've been updated for modern comfort, they still retain their timeless charm. The architecture of a riad is a harmonious blend of **Moorish, Berber, and Andalusian** influences, with a focus on natural materials, symmetry, and intricate detailing.

**Courtyards**: The heart of any riad is its central courtyard, which often features a **fountain** or **pool**, lush plants, and comfortable seating areas. Some courtyards are shaded by towering orange or palm trees, adding to the peaceful ambiance. The courtyard not only serves as a communal area for relaxation but also helps regulate the temperature, keeping the interior cool even in the heat of summer.

**Zellige Tiles**: One of the most striking features of a riad is its use of **zellige**—traditional Moroccan mosaic tilework. These tiles are arranged in intricate geometric patterns, creating colorful floors, walls, and fountains that are both decorative and functional. The zellige designs are often paired with **carved plasterwork**, adding further detail to the walls and arches.

**Woodwork**: Riads are also known for their beautifully carved **cedar wood ceilings** and **doors**, often intricately decorated with geometric and floral motifs. The woodwork, along with **stucco arabesques** and ornate lanterns, contributes to the sense of warmth and opulence that defines these homes.

**Roof Terraces**: Most riads feature **roof terraces**, offering panoramic views of the Medina, the **Atlas Mountains**, and the Marrakech skyline. These terraces are often furnished with lounge chairs and shaded seating areas, making them ideal spots for breakfast, evening drinks, or simply soaking in the views at sunset.

Staying in a Riad

For visitors, staying in a riad is more than just accommodation—it's an immersive experience in

Moroccan culture and hospitality. Most riads in Marrakech have been converted into **boutique hotels** or **guesthouses**, offering a personalized and intimate stay with modern comforts, while preserving their traditional charm.

**Personalized Service**: Riads are known for their warm, personalized service. Many are family-run, and hosts often go out of their way to make guests feel welcome, offering local tips, preparing traditional meals, and arranging excursions. This creates a homely, relaxed atmosphere, which stands in stark contrast to the often impersonal feel of larger hotels.

**Moroccan Cuisine**: Guests staying in a riad are often treated to delicious homemade Moroccan meals, including **tagines**, **couscous**, and fresh salads. Breakfast is typically served in the courtyard or on the terrace, and may include **mint tea**, fresh **pastries**, **fruit**, and **homemade jams**. Some riads also offer cooking classes, where guests can learn to prepare traditional Moroccan dishes using local ingredients.

**Peace and Privacy**: One of the greatest appeals of staying in a riad is the tranquility it offers. While the Medina outside may be full of activity, inside the riad, guests can enjoy peaceful courtyards, serene surroundings, and a sense of seclusion that makes it easy to unwind after a day of exploring.

Notable Riads in Marrakech

Marrakech is home to many beautifully restored riads, each with its own unique character and charm. Here are a few notable riads that have gained a reputation for their beauty, service, and atmosphere:

**Riad El Fenn**: Known for its artistic flair and eclectic design, Riad El Fenn combines traditional Moroccan elements with contemporary art. Its vibrant interiors, rooftop terrace, and serene courtyards make it a favorite among travelers looking for a stylish retreat in the heart of the Medina.

**Riad Kniza**: This luxury riad is known for its rich history and attention to detail. It has been meticulously restored, featuring traditional decor, zellige tiles, and cedar woodwork. The intimate atmosphere and exceptional service make it a top choice for those seeking an authentic Moroccan experience.

**Riad Yasmine**: One of the most Instagram-famous riads in Marrakech, Riad Yasmine is a visual delight with its emerald green pool, lush courtyard, and traditional Moroccan decor. Its intimate size and welcoming hosts create a laid-back and comfortable atmosphere.

**La Maison Arabe**: Originally founded in the 1940s as the first riad to offer cooking classes to foreigners, La

Maison Arabe has evolved into a luxury riad hotel. It features elegant rooms, a beautiful central pool, and one of the finest Moroccan restaurants in the city.

Visiting a Riad for Tea or Lunch

Even if you're not staying in a riad, many of these beautiful homes open their doors to non-residents for tea, lunch, or dinner. Enjoying a meal or a mint tea in the serene surroundings of a riad courtyard is a wonderful way to experience the tranquility of these hidden gems.

**Riad Dar Anika**: Located near the Royal Palace, Riad Dar Anika is known for its warm hospitality and traditional cuisine. It's a perfect spot for a relaxing lunch or afternoon tea, away from the bustle of the city.

**Le Jardin**: Although not a traditional riad, **Le Jardin** offers a similar experience, with its peaceful courtyard filled with plants and comfortable seating. It's a great place to escape the heat and enjoy a fresh juice or light meal.

The Legacy of Riads in Moroccan Culture

Riads have played a significant role in Moroccan culture for centuries, offering both a home and sanctuary for families within Medina. The preservation and restoration of these historic homes not only allow visitors to experience traditional Moroccan architecture but also help keep the city's cultural heritage alive.

Today, the riads of Marrakech stand as a testament to the beauty and ingenuity of Moroccan design. Whether you're staying in one for a few nights or simply visiting for an afternoon tea, the experience of stepping into a riad's serene courtyard offers a peaceful retreat and a lasting impression of Marrakech's rich cultural legacy.

## Gardens and Green Spaces

## Majorelle Garden: A Botanical Oasis

One of Marrakech's most beloved and iconic attractions, the **Majorelle Garden** (Jardin Majorelle) is a stunning botanical retreat nestled in the heart of the city. Known for its vibrant colors, exotic plants, and peaceful atmosphere, this garden offers visitors a refreshing escape from the hustle and bustle of the Medina. Created by French artist **Jacques Majorelle** in the 1920s and later restored by the famous fashion designer **Yves Saint Laurent**, Majorelle Garden is now one of the most visited sites in Marrakech, cherished for its beauty and serenity.

History of Majorelle Garden

Jacques Majorelle, a French Orientalist painter, fell in love with Morocco during the early 20th century and settled in Marrakech in 1917. He purchased a plot of land and began developing the garden in 1923. Over the next several decades, Majorelle transformed the space into a lush botanical haven, featuring exotic plants from around the world and a strikingly unique architectural style. His love for color, particularly the deep cobalt blue that now bears his name—**Majorelle Blue**—is evident throughout the garden, from the buildings to the fountains and planters.

Majorelle lived and worked on the property for many years, but after his death in 1962, the garden fell into disrepair. In the 1980s, fashion designer **Yves Saint Laurent** and his partner **Pierre Bergé** discovered the garden and decided to purchase and restore it to its former glory. They saved the garden from destruction and made it accessible to the public, turning it into one of Marrakech's most treasured landmarks.

Exploring the Majorelle Garden

Majorelle Garden is a visual feast, offering a vibrant mix of plant life, colorful structures, and serene water features. The garden's design reflects both Majorelle's artistic sensibilities and the influence of traditional Moroccan aesthetics.

**Majorelle Blue**: One of the most striking elements of the garden is its use of **Majorelle Blue**, a bold and vivid shade of cobalt that Jacques Majorelle incorporated into his art and architecture. This intense color is used throughout the garden, covering walls, fountains, planters, and the iconic **villa**, creating a stunning contrast against the greenery of the plants.

**Exotic Plant Collection**: Majorelle Garden is home to over **300 species of plants** from five continents, including towering palms, bamboo, cacti, and succulents. The layout of the garden is designed to create a feeling of harmony between the natural and the man-made, with winding pathways leading visitors through dense clusters of plants and open spaces that feel almost tropical.

**Water Features**: Fountains and water channels are an integral part of the garden's design, inspired by the traditional **Moorish** and **Islamic** gardens that use water as a symbol of life and refreshment. The soothing sound of trickling water adds to the tranquility of the space, making it an ideal spot for reflection and relaxation.

**Birdlife**: The garden also attracts various species of birds, making it a haven for birdwatchers. The quiet, lush environment provides an ideal home for local and migratory birds, which adds to the garden's peaceful atmosphere.

The Villa Oasis and Yves Saint Laurent

At the heart of Majorelle Garden stands the striking **Villa Oasis**, the former studio and home of Jacques Majorelle. Painted in vibrant Majorelle Blue, the villa is an architectural masterpiece and a key feature of the garden. Although the villa is not open to the public, it is an iconic focal point, surrounded by a landscape that complements its bold design.

The connection between Majorelle Garden and Yves Saint Laurent is inseparable. After Saint Laurent and

Pierre Bergé purchased the garden, it became one of their favorite retreats, and they spent much of their time here. Following Yves Saint Laurent's death in 2008, a **memorial** was created in the garden, featuring a simple column in his honor. His ashes were scattered in the garden, further solidifying his deep connection to this enchanting place.

The Berber Museum

Located within Majorelle Garden is the **Berber Museum**, a small but fascinating museum dedicated to the culture and history of Morocco's indigenous **Berber** people. Housed in the former artist's studio, the museum features a carefully curated collection of traditional Berber artifacts, including jewelry, textiles, and pottery, showcasing the rich heritage of the Berber communities from across Morocco.

**Exhibits**: The museum's exhibits highlight the artistry and craftsmanship of the Berber people, with displays of traditional garments, weapons, and ceremonial objects. The museum also explores the deep connection between the Berbers and the natural world, reflected in their use of natural dyes and materials.

**Visit**: The Berber Museum is a must-see for those interested in Moroccan culture and provides an insightful complement to the beauty of the garden itself.

Visiting Tips

**Best Time to Visit**: Majorelle Garden can get quite busy, especially during peak tourist seasons. To enjoy the garden at its most peaceful, visit early in the morning or late in the afternoon. The garden is open daily from 8 AM to 6 PM, with extended hours in the summer months.

**Photography**: Majorelle Garden is one of the most photogenic spots in Marrakech, with its vibrant colors, exotic plants, and unique architecture. Photography is allowed, but be respectful of other visitors when taking pictures.

**Tickets**: The entrance fee includes access to both the garden and the Berber Museum. Tickets can be purchased at the gate or in advance online to avoid long lines during busy times.

**Relaxation**: After exploring the garden, take a moment to relax at the on-site **café**, where you can enjoy refreshments in a tranquil setting. The café offers a selection of teas, juices, and light snacks, making it a perfect spot to unwind.

The Legacy of Majorelle Garden

Majorelle Garden is not only a botanical oasis but also a cultural icon that reflects the deep artistic and historical ties between Morocco and the world. The restoration of the garden by Yves Saint Laurent and Pierre Bergé ensured that this unique space would continue to inspire visitors with its beauty and tranquility.

For anyone visiting Marrakech, a trip to Majorelle Garden is an opportunity to step into a world of color, nature, and creativity. Whether you're admiring the striking Majorelle Blue, wandering through the lush greenery, or learning about Berber culture in the museum, the garden offers a peaceful retreat that will leave a lasting impression.

## Menara Gardens Serenity at the Foot of the Atlas Mountains

Just a short distance from the hustle and bustle of Marrakech's Medina lies the tranquil oasis of the **Menara Gardens**, offering visitors a peaceful retreat with stunning views of the majestic **Atlas Mountains** in the background. Established in the 12th century during the reign of the Almohad dynasty, the Menara Gardens have long served as a place of serenity and natural beauty, drawing locals and visitors alike to its serene olive groves, reflective pools, and sweeping landscapes.

History of Menara Gardens

The Menara Gardens were originally created in the 12th century by the **Almohad Sultan Abd al-Mu'min** as part of a larger agricultural project aimed at providing Marrakech with a reliable water supply and a place for leisure. The gardens were named after the pavilion at their center, which was added in the 19th century by **Sultan Abderrahmane of Morocco**. The pavilion, with its green-tiled roof, is one of the most iconic features of the gardens and is often depicted in postcards and paintings of the city.

The Menara Gardens were built around a vast **reflective pool** that was fed by a sophisticated system of underground channels (known as **khettaras**), designed to bring water from the Atlas Mountains to irrigate the olive groves. This ancient irrigation system is still in use today, allowing the olive trees to thrive in the otherwise arid landscape of Marrakech.

Exploring Menara Gardens

The Menara Gardens are a vast, open space, covering about 100 hectares of olive groves and orchards, with wide walkways and shaded areas perfect for a leisurely stroll or quiet contemplation. The gardens' simplicity and natural beauty create a serene atmosphere, making it an ideal escape from the city's heat and noise.

**The Reflective Pool**: At the heart of the gardens lies the large **reflective pool**, which was originally used to irrigate the surrounding groves. Today, the pool serves as a central feature of the gardens, with the historic **Menara Pavilion** on its edge. The calm waters of the pool perfectly mirror the pavilion and the snow-capped Atlas Mountains in the distance, creating a breathtaking scene that has inspired artists and photographers for centuries.

**The Menara Pavilion**: The pavilion, with its distinctive green-tiled roof, was built in the 19th century by Sultan Abderrahmane and served as a place for royal retreats. The pavilion's simple yet elegant design reflects the understated beauty of the gardens. While the interior is not always open to the public, the pavilion provides a stunning backdrop for photographs and a serene spot for quiet reflection.

**Olive Groves**: Surrounding the pool and pavilion are vast **olive groves**, with trees that are hundreds of years old. The olive trees provide shade and create a peaceful, meditative environment for walking and relaxing. During the olive harvest season, the gardens become a hub of activity as local farmers collect olives from the trees, continuing a tradition that dates back centuries.

Views of the Atlas Mountains

One of the most striking aspects of the Menara Gardens is the **panoramic view of the Atlas Mountains**. On clear days, the snow-capped peaks of the mountains provide a stunning contrast to the greenery of the olive groves and the still waters of the pool. The mountains seem to rise directly from the edge of the garden, making the Menara Gardens a favorite spot for both locals and tourists seeking a peaceful setting with a magnificent natural backdrop.

This view is particularly beautiful during the late afternoon or early evening, when the setting sun casts a golden light over the gardens, and the reflection of the mountains in the pool creates a picture-perfect scene.

Visiting Tips

**Best Time to Visit**: The Menara Gardens can be visited year-round, but the best time to experience the gardens is in the early morning or late afternoon when the light is soft, and the air is cooler. During the spring and autumn months, the views of the Atlas Mountains are especially clear, adding to the beauty of the landscape.

**Photography**: The Menara Gardens are a popular spot for photographers, thanks to the reflective pool and stunning views of the Atlas Mountains. Arriving during the golden hour (just after sunrise or before sunset) is the best time to capture the tranquil beauty of the gardens.

**Relax and Unwind**: The gardens are a perfect place for a leisurely walk or to simply sit and enjoy the peaceful surroundings. There are few vendors or distractions, making this a quieter, more contemplative spot compared to the bustling Medina.

**Picnic Spot**: Many locals come to the Menara Gardens for picnics, bringing blankets and enjoying a peaceful lunch under the shade of the olive trees. Visitors are welcome to do the same, making the gardens an ideal place for a relaxing break during a day of sightseeing.

Cultural Significance

Beyond its natural beauty, the Menara Gardens hold significant cultural and historical value. They were originally designed as a symbol of the Almohad dynasty's engineering and agricultural prowess, reflecting their mastery of water management in an arid climate. The khettara irrigation system, which brought water from the Atlas Mountains to sustain the gardens, is a remarkable feat of medieval engineering, and its continued use today highlights the gardens' enduring legacy.

The Menara Pavilion, while simple in design, also symbolizes the connection between the royal family and Marrakech's natural landscape. The pavilion was used by Sultan Abderrahmane as a retreat from the pressures of palace life, offering a serene setting for contemplation and relaxation. Over the centuries, the Menara Gardens have remained a beloved part of Marrakech's cultural heritage, treasured by locals and visitors alike for their beauty and tranquility.

The Legacy of Menara Gardens

For over 800 years, the Menara Gardens have been a peaceful oasis at the foot of the Atlas Mountains, offering a retreat from the city's heat and a place of quiet reflection. Today, the gardens continue to serve as a symbol of Marrakech's connection to the natural world, showcasing the enduring beauty of traditional Moroccan landscape design.

Whether you're walking through the olive groves, sitting by the reflective pool, or simply enjoying the stunning views of the Atlas Mountains, a visit to the Menara Gardens offers a moment of serenity and connection with nature. For those seeking a break from the hustle and bustle of Marrakech, this peaceful oasis provides the perfect escape.

# Culinary Delights

## Traditional Moroccan Dishes to Try

Morocco is famous for its rich and flavorful cuisine, a harmonious blend of Mediterranean, Berber, Arab, and African influences. The vibrant use of spices, fresh ingredients, and slow-cooking techniques has earned Moroccan food a global reputation for being both comforting and exotic. Whether you're dining in a bustling street market or at an upscale restaurant, these traditional Moroccan dishes are a must-try during your visit to Marrakech.

1. Tagine

Named after the distinctive clay pot in which it is cooked, **tagine** is arguably Morocco's most iconic dish. The slow-cooked stew is traditionally prepared with a variety of ingredients, including meat, vegetables, and fragrant spices. The unique shape of the tagine pot allows steam to circulate during cooking, making the food tender and flavorful.

**Common Varieties**:

**Lamb Tagine with Prunes**: A sweet and savory version made with tender lamb, prunes, almonds, and a touch of cinnamon, often garnished with sesame seeds.

**Chicken Tagine with Preserved Lemons and Olives**: This dish features chicken cooked with briny green olives and preserved lemons, giving it a zesty and tangy flavor.

**Vegetable Tagine**: A vegetarian option filled with seasonal vegetables, chickpeas, and a blend of aromatic spices such as cumin, coriander, and saffron.

Tagine is typically served with Moroccan **khobz** (flatbread), which is perfect for soaking up the flavorful sauce.

2. Couscous

Another staple of Moroccan cuisine is **couscous**, a dish made from semolina wheat that is steamed to a light, fluffy texture. Couscous is traditionally served on Fridays as a family meal after the midday prayers, but it's enjoyed throughout the week as well.

**Couscous with Seven Vegetables**: This classic version features a generous serving of couscous topped with a variety of vegetables, such as carrots, zucchini, potatoes, and squash, all cooked in a fragrant broth. It is often accompanied by lamb, chicken, or beef.

**Sweet Couscous (Seffa)**: A unique variation, sweet couscous is made with raisins, cinnamon, and powdered sugar, often served as a dessert or at special celebrations.

### 3. Pastilla

**Pastilla** (also known as **b'stilla**) is a savory-sweet pie made with delicate layers of **warqa** dough (similar to phyllo) and stuffed with a mixture of meat, usually pigeon or chicken, along with almonds, eggs, and fragrant spices. The filling is encased in crispy dough and dusted with powdered sugar and cinnamon, giving it a unique blend of sweet and savory flavors.

Originally from Fez, pastilla is often served as a starter at special occasions like weddings and banquets, but you can also find it at many restaurants in Marrakech.

### 4. Harira

A staple of Moroccan cuisine, **harira** is a hearty soup made with tomatoes, lentils, chickpeas, and fresh herbs, often thickened with flour. It's commonly eaten to break the fast during **Ramadan**, but it's enjoyed throughout the year as a comforting dish.

Harira is often served with **dates** and **chebakia** (a sweet, fried sesame cookie), making it a perfect meal for any time of day, especially during colder months.

### 5. Mechoui

**Mechoui** is Morocco's version of slow-roasted lamb, traditionally cooked in a clay oven or over an open flame until the meat is incredibly tender. The lamb is seasoned simply with cumin, salt, and sometimes saffron, allowing the rich flavors of the meat to shine.

Mechoui is often served at celebratory feasts or on special occasions, but you can find it at some restaurants, especially in Marrakech's **Jemaa el-Fnaa** square. The meat is typically served with flatbread and a sprinkle of cumin for dipping.

6. Zaalouk

**Zaalouk** is a popular Moroccan salad made from cooked eggplant, tomatoes, garlic, and spices, including cumin, paprika, and olive oil. The ingredients are mashed into a soft, creamy consistency and served warm or at room temperature.

Zaalouk is often served as a side dish with **khobz** (Moroccan bread) or as part of a mezze platter. Its smoky and tangy flavors make it a great complement to heavier dishes like tagine or couscous.

7. Moroccan Mint Tea

While not a dish, **Moroccan mint tea** (atay) is an essential part of Moroccan cuisine and hospitality. This refreshing drink is made with **green tea**, **fresh mint leaves**, and plenty of sugar, brewed and served from a height to create a frothy head in small, delicate glasses.

Moroccan mint tea is typically served after meals or during social gatherings and is often paired with **pastries** or **cookies**. Drinking tea is a ritual in Morocco, and it's common to enjoy several rounds, each poured from a height to aerate and mix the flavors.

8. Briouats

**Briouats** are small, triangular pastries made with **warqa** dough and filled with a variety of savory or sweet fillings. These bite-sized treats are often deep-fried to a crispy golden brown and served as an appetizer or snack.

**Savory Briouats**: These are typically filled with minced meat (lamb or chicken), cheese, and spices such as cinnamon and cumin.

**Sweet Briouats**: These are filled with almonds, honey, and cinnamon, making them a delicious dessert or snack with tea.

9. Tangia

A specialty of Marrakech, **tangia** is a slow-cooked stew made with lamb, garlic, preserved lemons, and spices such as cumin and saffron. The dish is traditionally cooked in a clay urn-like pot and buried in hot ashes, allowing the meat to become incredibly tender and infused with the flavors of the spices.

Tangia is unique to Marrakech and is often prepared for special occasions or communal meals. The dish is typically served with bread, and its rich, deep flavors make it a favorite among locals and visitors alike.

10. Chebakia

For those with a sweet tooth, **chebakia** is a popular Moroccan dessert, especially during Ramadan. These sesame-coated cookies are shaped into intricate patterns, deep-fried, and soaked in honey, giving them a crispy texture and sweet, sticky glaze.

Chebakia is often enjoyed with mint tea or alongside a bowl of harira soup, making it a delicious treat for any time of the day.

11. Maakouda

**Maakouda** are crispy Moroccan potato cakes, made from mashed potatoes mixed with garlic, parsley, and spices, then formed into patties and fried until golden. They are a popular street food in Marrakech and are often served in sandwiches or as a side dish to complement tagines or grilled meats.

These traditional Moroccan dishes offer a delicious introduction to the country's vibrant culinary heritage.

Whether you're enjoying a slow-cooked tagine, sipping on sweet mint tea, or indulging in a flaky pastry, the flavors of Morocco are sure to leave a lasting impression on your palate. Be sure to explore the local markets, street vendors, and restaurants to experience the full spectrum of Moroccan cuisine during your visit to Marrakech.

## The Best Restaurants and Street Food Spots

Marrakech is a culinary hotspot, offering a vibrant mix of high-end restaurants, cozy riads, and lively street food stalls. From traditional Moroccan dishes like tagine and couscous to innovative takes on classic flavors, the city's food scene is sure to impress both locals and travelers alike. Whether you're looking for an upscale dining experience or a taste of authentic street food, Marrakech has something to satisfy every palate.

1. Al Fassia

Known for its warm atmosphere and exceptional service, **Al Fassia** is one of the best places in Marrakech to enjoy authentic Moroccan cuisine. What makes this restaurant unique is that it is entirely run by women, from the chefs to the waitstaff. Located in the **Gueliz** district, Al Fassia offers a refined take on traditional dishes, including rich tagines, perfectly spiced couscous, and their signature roast lamb.

**Must-Try Dishes**: Lamb with prunes, chicken tagine with preserved lemons and olives, zaalouk (eggplant salad).

**Address**: 55 Boulevard Zerktouni, Gueliz.

2. La Maison Arabe

One of Marrakech's oldest and most iconic restaurants, **La Maison Arabe** offers a luxurious dining experience in a beautifully restored riad. The menu focuses on traditional Moroccan dishes, prepared with the highest quality ingredients and attention to detail. Guests can dine in the courtyard by candlelight, surrounded by the scent of jasmine and the sound of a trickling fountain.

**Must-Try Dishes**: Beef tagine with figs, chicken pastilla, and Moroccan mint tea.

**Address**: 1 Derb Assehbi, Bab Doukkala.

3. Nomad

Located in the heart of the **Medina**, **Nomad** is a contemporary restaurant with a modern twist on Moroccan cuisine. Its chic rooftop terrace offers stunning views of Marrakech, making it a favorite spot for both locals and tourists. The menu combines traditional Moroccan ingredients with international flavors, offering dishes like lamb burgers and quinoa salads alongside classic tagines.

**Must-Try Dishes**: Lamb burger, saffron chicken tagine, and spiced pumpkin soup.

**Address**: 1 Derb Aarjane, Rahba Kedima.

4. Le Jardin

Tucked away in Medina, **Le Jardin** is a peaceful oasis offering a blend of traditional and contemporary Moroccan cuisine. The restaurant is set in a lush, plant-filled courtyard, providing a relaxing retreat from the busy streets of Marrakech. Le Jardin is known for its laid-back atmosphere and fusion menu that caters to a range of dietary preferences, including vegetarian and gluten-free options.

**Must-Try Dishes**: Grilled kefta (spiced meatballs), fish tagine, and vegetable couscous.

**Address**: 32 Souk Jeld Sidi Abdelaziz, Medina.

5. Café Clock

For a more casual dining experience, **Café Clock** is a popular spot among locals and travelers alike. Known for its **camel burger**, this quirky café also offers a variety of traditional Moroccan and international dishes. Located near the **Kasbah**, Café Clock has a laid-back vibe, with live music, cooking classes, and cultural events held regularly.

**Must-Try Dishes**: Camel burger, harira soup, and date cake.

**Address**: 224 Derb Chtouka, Kasbah.

6. Dar Yacout

**Dar Yacout** offers a classic Moroccan dining experience in one of Marrakech's most beautiful settings. The restaurant, housed in a stunning traditional riad, is known for its elaborate multi-course meals and opulent décor. The experience starts with a selection of Moroccan salads, followed by hearty tagines, couscous, and roast meats. The rooftop terrace provides breathtaking views of Medina, especially at night when the city lights up.

**Must-Try Dishes**: Chicken tagine with saffron, lamb mechoui, and couscous with vegetables.

**Address**: 79 Sidi Ahmed Soussi, Medina.

7. Jemaa el-Fnaa Street Food Stalls

For an authentic street food experience, there's no better place than the lively stalls of **Jemaa el-Fnaa**, Marrakech's main square. As the sun sets, the square comes alive with smoke rising from the grills, the scent of spices filling the air, and vendors selling everything from grilled meats to spicy **snails**. Eating at these food stalls is an adventure in itself, offering a taste of Marrakech's vibrant street food culture.

**Must-Try Dishes**:

**Grilled Meats**: Skewers of marinated lamb, chicken, and kefta, often served with flatbread.

**Snails**: A Moroccan street food staple, cooked in a spiced broth that is rich with flavors like anise and cumin.

**Sheep's Head**: For the adventurous eater, try the slow-cooked sheep's head, a local delicacy served with cumin and salt.

**Harira**: A traditional soup made with tomatoes, lentils, chickpeas, and herbs, perfect for an evening snack.

8. Chez Lamine Hadj Mustapha

If you want to experience **mechoui** (slow-roasted lamb) the traditional way, **Chez Lamine Hadj Mustapha** is a must-visit. Located near Jemaa el-Fnaa, this humble spot is famous for its roasted lamb, cooked in underground ovens until the meat is tender and falls off the bone. The lamb is served with cumin and salt, and eaten with bread—a simple but deeply satisfying meal.

**Must-Try Dishes**: Mechoui (roasted lamb) and tangia (slow-cooked lamb stew).

**Address**: Rue Bani Marine, near Jemaa el-Fnaa.

9. Henna Art Café

For a mix of art, culture, and delicious food, **Henna Art Café** is a unique spot in the heart of Medina. This cozy café serves a variety of traditional Moroccan dishes alongside more international options, all in a relaxed, artistic setting. The café also offers henna tattoos, making it a fun and creative stop for tourists.

**Must-Try Dishes**: Chicken pastilla, zaalouk, and Moroccan mint tea with honey.

**Address**: 35 Derb Sqaya, Medina.

10. Mechoui Alley

Tucked away near the **Jemaa el-Fna** square, **Mechoui Alley** is a narrow street lined with small restaurants that specialize in traditional roasted lamb. The lamb is cooked in underground clay ovens, giving it a smoky flavor and incredibly tender texture. Served with a side of cumin and salt, this is a must-try for meat lovers visiting Marrakech.

**Must-Try Dishes**: Roasted lamb (mechoui) and lamb tangia.

**Address**: Off Jemaa el-Fnaa, near the Souks.

Insider Tips for Dining in Marrakech

**Portion Sizes**: Moroccan meals are often served in generous portions, especially in traditional restaurants. It's common to share dishes family-style, so consider ordering a few items to split among your group.

**Tipping**: In most restaurants and cafés, it is customary to leave a tip of 10% for good service. In street food stalls, rounding up your bill or leaving a few extra dirhams is appreciated.

**Vegetarian Options**: While Moroccan cuisine is often meat-heavy, there are plenty of vegetarian options available, including vegetable tagines, couscous, salads, and soups. Many restaurants, especially in more touristy areas, also cater to vegan and gluten-free diets.

## Moroccan Tea Culture and Café Scene

One of the most cherished aspects of Moroccan life is its rich and inviting tea culture. Known as **atay** in Arabic, Moroccan tea is more than just a beverage—it is a symbol of hospitality, friendship, and relaxation. Whether you're sitting in a bustling street café in Medina or enjoying tea in a quiet courtyard, sipping on a cup of **mint tea** (also known as **Moroccan whiskey**) is an essential part of the Moroccan experience. Coupled with the country's vibrant café scene, this tradition offers both locals and visitors a window into the social fabric of Morocco.

The Ritual of Moroccan Tea

Tea is at the heart of Moroccan culture, and the process of preparing and serving it is an art form in itself. The tea most commonly consumed in Morocco is a blend of **green tea**, usually **Chinese gunpowder tea**, with fresh **mint leaves** and plenty of **sugar**. This refreshing drink is consumed throughout the day, whether after a meal, during social gatherings, or simply to relax.

**The Art of Preparation**: Preparing Moroccan tea is a ritual that requires patience and precision. The tea is steeped in boiling water, and fresh mint leaves are added to the pot. Sugar is often included generously, though the amount can be adjusted to taste. The tea is traditionally served in small glasses, poured from a height to create a frothy "crown" on top. This technique also helps to mix the flavors and aerate the tea, enhancing its taste.

**Hospitality**: In Morocco, offering tea to guests is a sign of hospitality and respect. Whether you're visiting someone's home, a riad, or a café, you will almost always be greeted with a cup of tea. It's considered polite to accept, and it's common to enjoy at least two or three rounds. Refusing tea can be seen as impolite, so even if you're not a big tea drinker, accepting a small glass is part of the cultural exchange.

**Variations**: While the classic **mint tea** is the most popular, there are many regional variations. In the south of Morocco, for example, **absinthe** (known as **chiba**) is sometimes used instead of mint. During the colder months, tea may be made with warming spices like **cinnamon** or **sage**, adding a seasonal twist to the drink.

Moroccan Tea Traditions and Etiquette

Moroccan tea is more than just a beverage; it's a symbol of community and connection. There are a few customs and traditions that accompany tea drinking in Morocco, and understanding these can enhance your experience.

**Pouring Technique**: Tea is always poured from a height, a practice that is as much about flavor as it is about showmanship. This technique cools the tea slightly and aerates it, while also creating an attractive froth at the top of the glass. The higher the pour, the more experienced the tea server is considered to be.

**Serving Guests**: In Moroccan households, the host is responsible for making and serving tea to guests. It is customary to serve the eldest or most senior guest first, followed by others in descending order. When drinking tea, it's polite to take small sips and enjoy the tea slowly, as tea sessions often last for an extended period.

**Three Cups Tradition**: There's a popular saying in Morocco that "the first cup is as bitter as life, the second is as sweet as love, and the third is as gentle as death." This refers to the tradition of serving three rounds of tea during a sitting. Each cup has a slightly different flavor profile, with the first being the strongest and the third being the lightest, reflecting the changing strength of the mint leaves and tea as more water is added.

The Café Scene in Morocco

Cafés are an integral part of Moroccan daily life, particularly in Marrakech, where you can find both traditional **Moorish cafés** and modern establishments catering to a diverse crowd. The café scene offers a glimpse into the social culture of the country, where friends gather, business meetings take place, and people-watching becomes a leisurely activity.

**Café Culture**: Unlike in some Western countries, where cafés are often a quick stop for coffee or tea, Moroccan cafés are places to linger. It's common to see people spending hours chatting, playing cards, or simply watching the world go by. Cafés are particularly popular with men, and you'll often see groups of men gathering for tea or coffee, discussing everything from local politics to football.

**Café Noir and Espresso**: While tea is the star of Moroccan beverage culture, **coffee** is also widely consumed. The most popular style is **café noir**, a strong black coffee similar to espresso. For those who prefer something milder, **nous-nous**, which means "half-half," is a half-coffee, half-milk drink similar to a café au lait. Moroccan cafés offer a range of coffees, from simple espressos to more elaborate drinks like **café au lait** and **cappuccinos**, often served with a small glass of water or a sweet pastry.

**Café Design**: Traditional Moroccan cafés are typically simple and unpretentious, with tables and chairs set up outside to take advantage of the pleasant climate and allow for people-watching. The décor is usually understated, with wooden furniture and minimal embellishments. However, in cities like Marrakech, modern cafés have emerged that blend traditional Moroccan elements with contemporary design, offering comfortable seating, Wi-Fi, and international menus.

Must-Visit Cafés in Marrakech

Marrakech is home to a wide range of cafés, from traditional spots where locals gather to sip tea to modern establishments with rooftop terraces offering stunning views of the city. Here are a few notable cafés to visit:**Café des Épices**: Located in the heart of the Medina, **Café des Épices** is known for its rooftop terrace, offering sweeping views of the souks and the Atlas Mountains in the distance. The café serves both Moroccan tea and international coffee, along with light snacks. It's a popular spot for travelers looking to take a break from the hustle and bustle of the souks.

**Café de France**: A historic café located on the edge of **Jemaa el-Fnaa**, **Café de France** has been a gathering place for locals and tourists alike for decades. With its prime location, it offers excellent views of the square and is perfect for watching the lively street performers while sipping on a traditional Moroccan tea or coffee.

**Le Jardin**: Tucked away in the Medina, **Le Jardin** is a stylish café set in a lush courtyard filled with greenery. The café blends Moroccan design with a contemporary feel, offering a peaceful escape from the city's busy streets. Le Jardin serves a variety of teas, coffees, and traditional Moroccan dishes, making it a great spot for both lunch and a relaxing tea break.

**Nomad**: Another rooftop gem in Medina, **Nomad** is known for its modern twist on Moroccan cuisine and its laid-back atmosphere. It's a perfect spot to enjoy a leisurely tea while taking in the panoramic views of Marrakech's rooftops. Nomad's chic décor and relaxed vibe make it a favorite among travelers looking for a more modern take on the café experience.

Tea Beyond the Café: Moroccan Tea in Daily Life

While cafés are an important part of Moroccan social life, tea drinking is deeply embedded in everyday life at home. Families and friends gather for tea throughout the day, whether as part of a formal meal or simply to take a break from daily activities. In rural areas, tea is often served in elaborate tea sets with intricately designed teapots and glasses, reflecting the artistry that goes into every aspect of Moroccan tea culture.

Tea is also a staple during important celebrations and gatherings, such as weddings and holidays. It's an integral part of hospitality, with the act of serving tea symbolizing respect, friendship, and warmth.

The Legacy of Moroccan Tea Culture

Moroccan tea culture is more than just a tradition—it's a way of life that reflects the country's values of hospitality, community, and relaxation. Whether enjoyed in a bustling street café or in the quiet of a riad courtyard, Moroccan tea offers a moment of connection with both the people and the rich history of the country.

For visitors, taking part in the tea ritual is a way to experience the true essence of Morocco. Whether you're sipping mint tea in Medina or watching the world go by from a rooftop café, the simple act of sharing tea provides a unique glimpse into Moroccan life and its timeless traditions.

# Art and Culture

## Museums and Galleries: Marrakech Museum, Maison de la Photographie

Marrakech is a city steeped in history and culture, with a vibrant art scene that spans centuries. From traditional Berber artifacts to contemporary photography, the city's museums and galleries offer a fascinating glimpse into Morocco's artistic and cultural heritage. Two must-visit institutions are the **Marrakech Museum**, housed in a stunning former palace, and the **Maison de la Photographie**, a gallery dedicated to preserving Morocco's visual history through photography. Both spaces provide an immersive experience for those looking to explore the rich artistic traditions of Marrakech and Morocco as a whole.

Marrakech Museum

Located in the heart of Medina, the **Marrakech Museum** is housed in the magnificent **Dar Menebhi Palace**, a 19th-century building that was restored in the late 1990s. The museum offers visitors a journey through Moroccan art, culture, and history, featuring a diverse collection of artifacts, including traditional pottery, textiles, jewelry, and historical manuscripts. The building itself is a masterpiece of Moroccan architecture, making it as much a part of the experience as the exhibits it holds.

**The Palace Architecture**: The Dar Menebhi Palace is a stunning example of traditional **Andalusian-Moroccan architecture**, with a central courtyard adorned with a **zellige-tiled fountain**, intricate **stucco work**, and beautifully carved wooden doors. The palace's architecture is a reminder of the city's regal past, and visitors can easily spend time admiring the building's structure as much as the exhibits inside.

**Art and Exhibits**: The Marrakech Museum's collection spans centuries, with a mix of **contemporary Moroccan art**, **historic artifacts**, and rotating exhibitions. Highlights include traditional Moroccan crafts such as **ceramics**, **calligraphy**, and **metalwork**, as well as rare historical documents and **Koranic manuscripts**. The museum also hosts exhibitions featuring the works of local Moroccan artists, showcasing the country's thriving modern art scene.

**The Central Courtyard**: At the heart of the museum is the central courtyard, covered by an enormous **chandelier-like installation** that casts beautiful shadows across the space. The courtyard is a peaceful area where visitors can sit and enjoy the surroundings, reflecting the calm atmosphere of a traditional Moroccan riad.

**Visiting Tips**:

**Location**: Dar Menebhi, Place Ben Youssef, Medina.

**Hours**: Open daily, typically from 9:00 AM to 6:00 PM.

**Nearby Attractions**: The museum is located near the **Ben Youssef Madrasa** and the **Almoravid Koubba**, making it a convenient stop while exploring the historic center of Marrakech.

Maison de la Photographie

For a unique glimpse into Morocco's past through the lens of photography, a visit to the **Maison de la Photographie** is a must. This charming gallery is housed in a restored riad in Medina and is dedicated to showcasing the history of Morocco through a vast collection of photographs, postcards, and prints, dating from the 19th century to the present day. The gallery offers a rare and intimate look at Morocco's people, landscapes, and culture as they have evolved over the years.

**A Historical Journey Through Photography**: Maison de la Photographie features an extensive archive of photographs taken throughout Morocco over the past 150 years. The collection includes portraits of Berber villagers, landscapes of the Atlas Mountains, and scenes from daily life in Marrakech and other cities. These images provide a rare and valuable record of Morocco's cultural diversity and historical changes, offering insight into the lives of the country's people through different eras.

**Themed Exhibitions**: The gallery frequently rotates its exhibitions, often focusing on specific themes such as **Berber culture**, **early 20th-century explorers**, or **Marrakech in the early 1900s**. The photographs on display range from candid snapshots of daily life to formal portraits and documentary images that capture pivotal moments in Moroccan history.

**Roof Terrace**: After viewing the photographs, visitors can head up to the gallery's **rooftop terrace**, which offers panoramic views of the Medina and the Atlas Mountains. The terrace is a peaceful spot to reflect on the exhibits while enjoying a cup of Moroccan tea or coffee.

**Visiting Tips**:

**Location**: 46 Rue Ahl Fes, Medina.

**Hours**: Open daily, typically from 9:30 AM to 6:00 PM.

**Nearby Attractions**: Maison de la Photographie is located near the **Marrakech Museum** and the **Ben Youssef Madrasa**, making it easy to visit several cultural sites in one day.

Exploring Marrakech's Art and Culture

Both the Marrakech Museum and Maison de la Photographie provide an immersive experience for those looking to dive deeper into Moroccan art and history. While the Marrakech Museum offers a broad overview of traditional and modern Moroccan art, Maison de la Photographie focuses on preserving the visual history of Morocco, highlighting the power of photography to capture the country's diverse culture and landscapes.

For art lovers and history enthusiasts alike, these two institutions offer a perfect blend of traditional craftsmanship, historical insights, and contemporary artistic expression, making them essential stops on any cultural tour of Marrakech.

## Traditional Arts and Crafts Carpets, Pottery, and Jewelry

Marrakech is a city known for its vibrant artisanal traditions, where craftsmanship has been passed down through generations. From intricately woven carpets to hand-painted pottery and exquisitely crafted jewelry, the city offers a rich array of traditional Moroccan arts and crafts. These crafts are not just beautiful souvenirs but also a reflection of Morocco's diverse cultural heritage, deeply rooted in Berber, Arab, and Andalusian influences. As you explore the souks and artisan workshops, you'll encounter masterpieces that tell the story of Morocco's artistry, skill, and creative spirit.

1. Carpets

One of Morocco's most prized traditional crafts is its **hand woven carpets**, which have been produced by Berber tribes for centuries. These carpets are not only decorative but also carry cultural and symbolic significance, with each tribe and region having its own distinct style, patterns, and color schemes.

**Berber Carpets**: **Berber carpets** are known for their simple, geometric designs and natural, earthy colors. The most famous type is the **Beni Ourain rug**, typically woven from sheep's wool in neutral tones like cream, black, and brown. These rugs feature minimalist diamond or zigzag patterns and are often prized for their softness and durability. Each Berber carpet is unique, with the patterns often representing aspects of tribal life, such as fertility, protection, or nature.

**Zanafi Rugs**: Originating from the **Atlas Mountains**, **Zanafi rugs** are recognizable by their bold, linear patterns and monochrome color palettes. These flat-weave rugs are popular for their modern aesthetic and versatility.

**Colorful Kilims**: Another popular Moroccan carpet is the **kilim**, a flat-woven rug known for its bright colors and intricate patterns. Unlike Berber rugs, kilims are often woven with intricate floral or geometric designs in vibrant hues of red, orange, blue, and green. These rugs are particularly popular in regions like **Fez** and **Rabat**, where the influence of Arab and Andalusian craftsmanship is more pronounced.

**Buying Tips**: When shopping for a Moroccan carpet, it's important to understand the differences between handmade and machine-made rugs. Handmade carpets often have slight imperfections, which add to their charm and uniqueness, while machine-made rugs will have perfectly uniform designs. Bargaining is also an essential part of the purchasing process, so don't hesitate to negotiate with the vendor.

2. Pottery

Moroccan **pottery** is celebrated for its rich colors, intricate patterns, and practical beauty. Pottery is an integral part of daily life in Morocco, used for everything from serving food to decorating homes. Each region of Morocco has its own distinct pottery style, with **Fez** and **Safi** being two of the most well-known centers for this craft.

**Fez Pottery**: The city of **Fez** is renowned for its finely painted pottery, which is often decorated with traditional **zellige** patterns in shades of cobalt blue, green, and yellow. Fez pottery is typically made from high-quality clay, and the pieces are known for their delicate, symmetrical designs. Common items include bowls, plates, tagine pots, and vases, all featuring intricate geometric and floral motifs.

**Safi Pottery**: **Safi**, a coastal town, is another major center of Moroccan pottery. The pottery from Safi is characterized by its bold colors and more rustic designs. Many of the pieces from this region feature vibrant glazes in rich hues of red, green, and blue, and they often include traditional Berber symbols. Safi is particularly famous for its large, hand-thrown pots and tagines.

**Tagines**: One of the most iconic Moroccan pottery items is the **tagine**, a conical cooking vessel used to prepare the famous slow-cooked stews of the same name. Tagines are not only functional but also decorative, with many featuring hand-painted designs that make them a beautiful addition to any kitchen or dining table.

**Buying Tips**: When pOne of the most important decisions when planning your trip to Marrakech is choosing the perfect accommodation. The city offers a wide variety of lodging options, but two types stand out: **roads** and **hotels**. Each offers a distinct experience, and deciding between them will depend on your personal preferences, travel style, and the kind of atmosphere you're looking for. This chapter explores the differences between roads and hotels to help you decide where to stay in Marrakech.

1. What Is a Road?

A **riad** is a traditional Moroccan house or palace with a central courtyard or garden. The word "riad" comes from the Arabic word for "garden," and this design reflects a focus on creating an inward-facing sanctuary, providing peace and privacy from the busy streets outside. Many roads are located in Medina, the historic part of the city, and have been beautifully restored and converted into boutique guesthouses.

**Architectural Features**: Riads are known for their traditional Moroccan architecture, including **zellige tilework**, **carved woodwork**, and intricate **plaster decorations**. The central courtyard, often featuring a fountain or small pool, serves as a peaceful retreat for guests to relax and escape the hustle and bustle of the city. Many roads also have **rooftop terraces**, offering stunning views of the Medina and the distant Atlas Mountains.

**Personalized Service**: One of the main attractions of staying in a riad is the intimate and personalized experience. Roads are typically smaller than hotels, often with only a handful of rooms, allowing for a more tailored guest experience. Many roads are family-owned, and the hosts often go above and beyond to make guests feel welcome, offering home-cooked breakfasts, personalized recommendations, and a warm, friendly atmosphere.

**Cultural Immersion**: Staying in a riad allows you to experience Morocco's rich culture and heritage firsthand. The traditional decor, the layout, and even the meals are designed to reflect Moroccan customs and hospitality. For travelers looking to immerse themselves in the local culture, a riad offers an authentic experience.

2. What Is a Hotel?

While riads offer a traditional Moroccan experience, **hotels** in Marrakech range from luxurious international chains to modern boutique properties. Hotels can be found both in the heart of Medina and in the more modern neighborhoods of **Gueliz** and **Hivernage**, offering a different kind of stay with more standardized amenities and services.

**Range of Amenities**: Hotels often provide a wider range of amenities compared to riads, including **swimming pools**, **fitness centers**, **spas**, **restaurants**, and sometimes even nightclubs or bars. For travelers seeking a more resort-like experience, complete with modern conveniences, hotels may be the better option. Many luxury hotels in Marrakech, such as the **Four Seasons**, **Mandarin Oriental**, and **La Mamounia**, offer world-class facilities, including expansive pools, high-end spas, and gourmet dining.

**Larger Capacity**: Hotels generally have more rooms than riads, making them ideal for larger groups, families, or business travelers. The staff in hotels are usually trained to cater to a diverse range of guests, ensuring a high level of professionalism and service. However, this can sometimes mean a less personal experience compared to staying in a riad.

**Modern Design**: While many hotels incorporate Moroccan design elements, they also offer modern, international-style decor and layouts. Rooms are typically larger, with contemporary furnishings and high-tech amenities like **flat-screen TVs**, **Wi-Fi**, and **air conditioning**. For travelers who prefer a more cosmopolitan feel or need certain comforts, hotels can provide these with ease.

3. The Benefits of Staying in a Riad

For travelers seeking a more intimate, culturally rich experience, staying in a riad offers several unique benefits:

**Authenticity and Charm**: The charm of a riad lies in its authentic Moroccan architecture, decor, and atmosphere. Each riad is unique, offering a personalized experience that transports you into the heart of Moroccan history and culture. Many guests appreciate the peaceful retreat a riad provides after a day of exploring the lively streets of the Medina.

**Proximity to the Medina**: Most riads are located within the Medina, meaning you're just steps away from Marrakech's famous souks, historical sites, and bustling squares like **Jemaa el-Fnaa**. Staying in a riad allows you to fully experience the rhythm of the Medina, with easy access to its narrow alleyways, markets, and restaurants.

**Quiet and Relaxing Ambiance**: Despite being in the heart of the city, riads offer a quiet and serene environment. The inward-facing design blocks out the noise of the streets, creating a tranquil space for relaxation. The central courtyards, often filled with plants and the sound of running water, add to the peaceful ambiance.

**Personal Touch**: The small size and intimate nature of riads mean that the service is often more personalized. Many riads offer traditional Moroccan meals made from fresh, local ingredients, and some even provide cooking classes or other cultural experiences. The hosts are often more involved in making sure you have a memorable stay.

4. The Benefits of Staying in a Hotel

Hotels, especially luxury and boutique options, come with their own set of advantages, making them an attractive choice for travelers who prioritize convenience, amenities, and a modern feel:

**Full-Service Amenities**: Hotels often have a range of facilities, including pools, spas, gyms, and restaurants, giving guests everything they need for a comfortable and relaxing stay. For those who want to indulge in **luxury spa treatments**, enjoy **fine dining**, or simply relax by a large pool, hotels can provide these conveniences all in one place.

**Modern Comforts**: Hotels tend to offer more modern amenities, such as **room service**, **business centers**, and state-of-the-art technology. If you're traveling for business or simply prefer a more contemporary style, hotels are better suited to provide these comforts.

**Consistent Service**: Hotels are known for their consistency in service and quality. With international standards, many luxury hotels in Marrakech offer the kind of reliability and professionalism that international travelers expect. Whether it's housekeeping, concierge services, or on-site dining, hotels tend to be more predictable in their offerings.

**Variety of Locations**: While many roads are concentrated in Medina, hotels can be found throughout the city, including in the modern districts of Gueliz and Hivernage. These areas offer a more cosmopolitan experience, with wide boulevards, upscale restaurants, and shopping malls, providing a different perspective on Marrakech.

5. Which Is Right for You?

The choice between staying in a riad or a hotel comes down to your personal travel style and the type of experience you want to have in Marrakech.

**Choose a Riad If You Want**:

An authentic and immersive Moroccan experience.

To stay in a traditional setting with cultural charm.

Personalized service and a quieter, more intimate atmosphere.

To be close to Medina and its attractions.

**Choose a Hotel If You Want**:

Modern amenities and conveniences, such as pools, spas, and gyms.

A larger space with consistent, high-quality service.

Access to on-site restaurants, bars, and international dining options.

A more cosmopolitan stay in districts like Gueliz or Hivernage.

6. Top Recommendations

Here are a few of the top riads and hotels in Marrakech, known for their exceptional service and unique atmosphere:

**Top Riads**:

**Riad El Fenn**: A chic, boutique riad with luxurious rooms, a rooftop terrace, and a stylish blend of modern and traditional decor.

**Riad Kniza**: A beautifully restored 18th-century riad known for its authentic Moroccan atmosphere, personalized service, and traditional cuisine.

**Riad Yasmine**: Famous for its Instagram-worthy courtyard and pool, Riad Yasmine offers a serene and trendy escape in the heart of Medina.

**Top Hotels**:

**La Mamounia**: A world-renowned luxury hotel offering opulent rooms, a lavish spa, and stunning gardens, often regarded as one of the best hotels in the world.

**Four Seasons Resort Marrakech**: A modern, family-friendly resort with large pools, excellent dining options, and beautiful views of the Atlas Mountains.

**Es Saadi Palace**: A luxury hotel and spa located in the Hivernage district, offering a mix of Moroccan charm and modern amenities, including a casino and several restaurants.

Finding Your Perfect Stay

Whether you choose a traditional riad or a modern hotel, both options offer something special in Marrakech. Riads provide a unique, intimate experience steeped in Moroccan culture, while hotels offer modern comforts and a wide range of amenities. No matter where you stay, Marrakech's hospitality will ensure that your visit is unforgettable.

purchasing Moroccan pottery, look for pieces that are both decorative and functional. Handmade items will have subtle variations in glaze and design, which add to their charm. Be sure to ask the vendor if the piece is food-safe, especially if you plan to use it for cooking or serving.

3. Jewelry

Moroccan **jewelry** is known for its bold, intricate designs, often made with silver and adorned with colorful stones, enamel, and symbols. Jewelry has long played an important role in Moroccan culture, particularly in Berber communities, where it is worn not just for adornment but also as a symbol of wealth, status, and protection.

**Berber Jewelry**: Traditional **Berber jewelry** is typically made from silver, rather than gold, and is often decorated with coral, amber, turquoise, and lapis lazuli. These pieces are known for their large, bold designs, often featuring geometric shapes, symbolic patterns, and protective motifs like the **Hand of Fatima (Hamsa)** or **eye talismans** to ward off evil. Berber necklaces, bracelets, and earrings are often oversized and designed to make a statement, and they remain highly prized for their cultural significance and beauty.

**Enamel and Filigree Work**: Moroccan jewelers are skilled in a variety of techniques, including **filigree work**, where delicate metal threads are twisted into intricate designs, and **enamel work**, which involves fusing colored glass or gemstones to the surface of the metal. These techniques are often used to create elaborate pendants, earrings, and rings, which are popular with both locals and visitors.

**Silver Souks**: The **silver souks** of Marrakech are the best places to find authentic Moroccan jewelry. Located in Medina, these small workshops and stalls offer a wide range of handmade pieces, from traditional Berber designs to more modern interpretations of Moroccan jewelry. Bargaining is expected, so be prepared to negotiate the price.

**Buying Tips**: When purchasing Moroccan jewelry, look for hallmarks or stamps that indicate the metal's authenticity. Silver is often stamped with "925" to indicate its purity. Be sure to inspect the craftsmanship closely, as handmade pieces will have slight variations that machine-made items lack.

Exploring Traditional Moroccan Crafts

Whether you're wandering through the souks of Marrakech or visiting artisan cooperatives in the surrounding regions, Morocco's traditional arts and crafts offer a fascinating window into the country's rich cultural heritage. Each handcrafted item, whether it's a Berber carpet, a piece of pottery, or a silver bracelet, carries with it the legacy of centuries-old traditions and the skill of the artisans who created it.

For visitors, buying traditional Moroccan crafts is not only a way to take home a piece of Morocco but also a way to support local artisans and keep these ancient crafts alive. From the intricacy of a handwoven rug to the delicate artistry of a silver necklace, Moroccan crafts are truly a reflection of the country's history, creativity, and enduring sense of style.

**Festivals and Cultural Events:** When to Visit for Special Occasions

Marrakech is a city that celebrates its rich cultural heritage and vibrant traditions through a variety of festivals and events held throughout the year. These festivals, many of which are deeply rooted in Morocco's history, provide an opportunity for visitors to experience the music, art, food, and traditions that make the city so unique. From grand religious celebrations to contemporary arts festivals, Marrakech offers a diverse calendar of events that showcase the city's dynamic spirit. If you're planning a visit, timing your trip to coincide with one of these special occasions can offer a deeper, more immersive experience of the city.

1. Marrakech International Film Festival (Festival International du Film de Marrakech)

The **Marrakech International Film Festival** is one of the most prestigious cultural events in Morocco, attracting filmmakers, actors, and cinema enthusiasts from around the world. Held annually in December, this festival transforms Marrakech into a global stage for film, with screenings, panel discussions, and award ceremonies.

**What to Expect**: The festival showcases films from a wide range of genres and countries, often focusing on emerging filmmakers and innovative cinema. Many of the screenings take place at historic venues like the **Palais des Congrès** or in open-air settings at **Jemaa el-Fnaa**. The festival's glamorous red carpet events and star-studded guest list make it an exciting time to visit Marrakech for movie lovers.

**When**: Early December.

2. Eid al-Fitr and Eid al-Adha

Two of the most significant religious festivals in Morocco are **Eid al-Fitr** and **Eid al-Adha**, both of which mark important moments in the Islamic calendar.

These festivals are deeply spiritual and are celebrated with special prayers, family gatherings, and feasts.

**Eid al-Fitr**: This festival marks the end of **Ramadan**, the Islamic month of fasting. After a month of abstaining from food and drink during daylight hours, Eid al-Fitr is a time for joyous celebration, with families gathering for special meals, the giving of gifts, and charitable donations. Visitors in Marrakech during Eid al-Fitr can witness the city's mosques filled with worshippers and enjoy the festive atmosphere as locals don new clothes and visit family and friends.

**Eid al-Adha**: Also known as the **Festival of Sacrifice**, Eid al-Adha commemorates the willingness of the Prophet Ibrahim to sacrifice his son in obedience to God. This festival is marked by the ritual sacrifice of an animal, usually a sheep, and the distribution of meat to family, friends, and the less fortunate. Visitors may notice a quieter, more reflective mood during this holiday, as it is a time for prayer and family gatherings.

**When**: The dates for both Eids are based on the Islamic lunar calendar and vary each year.

3. Marrakech Popular Arts Festival (Festival National des Arts Populaires)

The **Marrakech Popular Arts Festival** is one of the city's oldest and most vibrant cultural events, celebrating Morocco's rich traditions of music, dance, and folklore. Held every summer, the festival brings together performers from all over the country, including Berber, Arab, and Gnawa musicians, as well as dancers and storytellers.

**What to Expect**: The festival is a colorful celebration of Morocco's cultural diversity, with performances taking place in iconic locations such as the **El Badi Palace** and the **Jemaa el-Fnaa** square. Visitors can enjoy a wide range of traditional performances, from **acrobats and fire-eaters** to **Gnawa musicians** and **Berber storytellers**. It's a fantastic way to experience Morocco's living traditions and to see the city come alive with music and dance.

**When**: July.

4. Marrakech Biennale

The **Marrakech Biennale** is an international festival dedicated to contemporary art, literature, and film, held every two years. This event has gained international recognition for its innovative exhibitions and installations, which transform the city into an open-air gallery of modern artistic expression. The biennale is a major draw for art lovers, offering a platform for artists from Morocco and around the world to showcase their work.

**What to Expect**: The festival includes a variety of contemporary art exhibitions, public performances, film screenings, and literary discussions. These events take place in some of Marrakech's most beautiful locations, including the **Bahia Palace**, the **Dar Si Said Museum**, and public spaces throughout the Medina. The biennale's focus on contemporary themes and global issues makes it an important event in the international art world.

**When**: Every two years, typically in February or March.

5. Moussem of Sidi Bel Abbas

The **Moussem of Sidi Bel Abbas** is a traditional religious festival that honors one of Marrakech's most important spiritual figures, **Sidi Bel Abbas**, the patron saint of the city. Sidi Bel Abbes is revered for his work with the poor and blind, and his mausoleum in the Medna is one of the most important pilgrimage sites in the city.

**What to Expect**: The moussem, or pilgrimage, is a time of religious devotion and celebration, with processions, prayers, and rituals taking place at the saint's mausoleum. While the event is primarily spiritual in nature, it also features traditional music, food, and the gathering of religious leaders and pilgrims from across the country. Visitors are welcome to observe the festivities, but it's important to be respectful of the religious significance of the event.

**When**: October.

6. Gnawa and World Music Festival (Essaouira)

Although held in the coastal town of **Essaouira**, just a few hours from Marrakech, the **Gnawa and World Music Festival** is a major cultural event that draws visitors from across Morocco and beyond. This annual festival celebrates the spiritual music of the **Gnawa people**, a mystical Sufi order with roots in West Africa, blending traditional rhythms with modern influences.

**What to Expect**: The festival brings together a diverse lineup of musicians, including traditional Gnawa performers, as well as international artists from genres like jazz, reggae, and world music. Held in the atmospheric squares and streets of Essaouira, this festival is a great opportunity to experience the soulful rhythms of Gnawa music in a relaxed and festive environment. Many visitors to Marrakech plan day trips or overnight stays in Essaouira to enjoy this unique musical event.

**When**: June.

7. Imilchil Marriage Festival

The **Imilchil Marriage Festival** is a unique cultural event that takes place in the Atlas Mountains, several hours from Marrakech. This festival, rooted in Berber tradition, is a large gathering where unmarried men and women from the surrounding tribes meet with the hope of finding a spouse. The festival is a rare opportunity to witness the rich cultural heritage of the **Berber people**, with traditional music, dancing, and rituals playing a key role in the festivities.

**What to Expect**: The festival is known for its lively atmosphere, with participants dressed in their finest traditional attire. The highlight of the event is the marriage ceremonies, where couples who have met at previous festivals officially tie the knot. Visitors can observe the colorful celebrations, enjoy traditional Berber music and food, and experience the hospitality of the local community.

**When**: Late August or September.

When to Visit for Festivals

If you're planning a trip to Marrakech and want to experience one of the city's vibrant festivals, timing is key. While the summer months are filled with music and arts festivals, the cooler months of fall and winter offer religious celebrations and film events. Regardless of when you visit, Marrakech's lively festival scene ensures that there is always something special happening to make your trip even more memorable.

## The Modern Side of Marrakech

### Gueliz and Hivernage: Modern Neighborhoods and Luxurious Living

While Marrakech is best known for its ancient Medina, souks, and centuries-old architectural wonders, the city also boasts a more contemporary side. The neighborhoods of **Gueliz** and **Hivernage** are the heart of modern Marrakech, offering a blend of luxury, chic cafés, upscale shopping, and vibrant nightlife. These districts reflect the city's evolution, combining Moroccan charm with European influences and modern living, making them popular areas for both locals and visitors seeking a more cosmopolitan experience.

1. Gueliz: The Trendy Hub of Marrakech

Gueliz, also known as the **Ville Nouvelle** (New City), was established during the French colonial period and has since become one of Marrakech's most vibrant and cosmopolitan districts. With its wide boulevards, trendy boutiques, and diverse selection of restaurants and cafés, Gueliz offers a stark contrast to the historic Medina.

**Shopping in Gueliz**: Gueliz is known for its modern shopping scene, with a mix of international brands and Moroccan designers. **Avenue Mohammed V**, the main thoroughfare, is lined with boutiques selling everything from high-end fashion to unique Moroccan handicrafts. For visitors looking to take home a piece of Marrakech's contemporary art scene, Gueliz is also home to several art galleries, including **Matisse Art Gallery** and **David Bloch Gallery**, showcasing the works of local and international artists.

**Dining and Cafés**: Gueliz is a culinary hotspot, offering a wide range of dining options that cater to both Moroccan and international tastes. Trendy cafés like **Café de la Poste** and **16 Café** are popular for their chic interiors and relaxed vibe, perfect for a leisurely breakfast or afternoon coffee. For fine dining, **Le Grand Café de la Poste** blends colonial-era charm with gourmet Moroccan and French cuisine, making it a must-visit for food lovers.

**Nightlife**: Gueliz comes alive at night with its lively bar and club scene. Whether you're looking to sip cocktails on a rooftop bar or dance the night away, the district has something for everyone. Popular spots like **Kechmara** and **L'envers** offer laid-back atmospheres, while more upscale venues like **Lotus Club** provide a glamorous night out.

**Cultural Attractions**: Beyond shopping and dining, Gueliz is also home to several cultural sites. The **Jardin Majorelle**, one of the most famous gardens in Morocco, is located at the edge of Gueliz and offers visitors a serene escape filled with vibrant colors, exotic plants, and the Yves Saint Laurent Museum. The museum celebrates the iconic designer's love for Marrakech and his contributions to the world of fashion.

2. Hivernage: Luxury and Leisure

Adjacent to Gueliz, the **Hivernage** district is synonymous with luxury living. Known for its wide, tree-lined streets and grand hotels, Hivernage is where you'll find Marrakech's most exclusive accommodations, high-end restaurants, and luxury spas. This upscale neighborhood is perfect for those looking to indulge in the finer things while enjoying the city's modern comforts.

**Luxury Hotels and Resorts**: Hivernage is home to some of the city's most prestigious hotels and resorts, including the **Four Seasons Resort Marrakech**, the **Es Saadi Palace**, and the legendary **La Mamounia**. These hotels offer world-class amenities, including luxurious spas, fine dining, and lush gardens, making them ideal retreats for those seeking relaxation and refinement. The rooftop bars at many of these hotels, such as the one at **Nobu Hotel**, offer panoramic views of the city and the Atlas Mountains.

**Fine Dining**: Hivernage is also a culinary destination, with a selection of high-end restaurants that offer a range of international and Moroccan cuisine. Restaurants like **Le Palace** and **Comptoir Darna** are known for their gourmet dishes and sophisticated ambiance, often combining dinner with live entertainment, including belly dancing and traditional Moroccan music. For a more relaxed but equally delicious experience, **Buddha-Bar Marrakech** offers a fusion of Asian and Moroccan cuisine in a chic, contemporary setting.

**Wellness and Spas**: The luxurious hotels in Hivernage also house some of the city's best spas, offering visitors the chance to unwind with traditional **hammam** treatments, massages, and beauty therapies. The spa at **La Mamounia** is particularly famous, combining opulent décor with world-class treatments in an oasis of calm.

**Nightlife and Entertainment**: Hivernage offers a more upscale nightlife scene compared to Gueliz, with a range of chic bars, rooftop lounges, and exclusive nightclubs. **So Lounge** at the Sofitel and **Theatro** are popular spots for those looking to experience Marrakech's glamorous nightlife, with international DJs and a lively, cosmopolitan crowd.

**Leisure and Green Spaces**: Despite its modernity, Hivernage retains a connection to nature, with several green spaces and parks. The **Cyber Park Arsat Moulay Abdeslam**, located at the edge of Hivernage, is a beautiful park where visitors can stroll among manicured gardens and historic buildings. The nearby **Menara Gardens** offer a larger, more tranquil space with stunning views of the Atlas Mountains.

What to Expect from Gueliz and Hivernage

**Modern Architecture**: Both Gueliz and Hivernage feature modern, European-inspired architecture, reflecting the French influence during the colonial period. You'll find wide boulevards, art deco buildings, and contemporary structures, contrasting with the more traditional architecture of the Medina.

**Contemporary Vibe**: These neighborhoods cater to a more cosmopolitan crowd, with an emphasis on style, luxury, and convenience. Expect trendy boutiques, upscale restaurants, and sleek hotels that cater to international tastes, making them ideal for travelers seeking modern comforts.

**Accessibility**: Gueliz and Hivernage are both centrally located and easily accessible from the Medina and other parts of Marrakech. Whether you're walking or taking a taxi, you can easily explore these neighborhoods alongside the city's historic areas.

When to Visit

If you're interested in experiencing the modern side of Marrakech, Gueliz and Hivernage are vibrant year-round. The cooler months from **October to April** are ideal for enjoying outdoor terraces, rooftop bars, and the neighborhood's parks and gardens. These months also coincide with many cultural events and festivals, making it a great time to explore all that these modern districts have to offer.

A Different Side of Marrakech

Gueliz and Hivernage provide a window into the modern, cosmopolitan side of Marrakech. Whether you're shopping in trendy boutiques, dining at world-class restaurants, or relaxing in luxury hotels, these neighborhoods offer a perfect complement to the city's historic Medina. For visitors looking to experience the best of both worlds, exploring the modern neighborhoods of Marrakech is a must.

## Shopping Beyond the Medina: Boutiques and Designer Stores

While Medina's bustling souks offer an authentic shopping experience filled with artisanal crafts, traditional textiles, and spices, Marrakech's modern side presents a different kind of retail therapy. The city's trendy neighborhoods, particularly **Gueliz** and **Hivernage**, are home to a growing number of chic boutiques, high-end designer stores, and concept shops. Here, you'll find a mix of Moroccan craftsmanship with a contemporary twist, as well as international fashion, luxury brands, and unique home décor. Shopping beyond the Medina allows visitors to discover Marrakech's modern fashion scene and upscale offerings, perfect for those looking to bring home something stylish and unique.

1. 33 Rue Majorelle

Located near the famous **Jardin Majorelle**, **33 Rue Majorelle** is one of Marrakech's most popular concept stores, offering a curated selection of Moroccan-designed fashion, accessories, and home goods. The boutique features work from over 70 Moroccan designers, making it a great spot to discover contemporary Moroccan style.

**What to Find**: 33 Rue Majorelle showcases a wide range of items, from handmade leather goods and contemporary jewelry to modern ceramics and home décor. You'll also find a selection of Moroccan-inspired fashion, including kaftans, scarves, and accessories, all with a modern twist.

**Location**: 33 Rue Yves Saint Laurent, Gueliz.

2. Moor

For those looking to explore the intersection of traditional Moroccan craftsmanship and modern design, **Moor** is a boutique that offers stylish home décor and accessories with a contemporary edge. Located in the heart of Gueliz, Moor's minimalist aesthetic makes it a favorite among design lovers.

**What to Find**: Moor specializes in high-end home décor, including handwoven rugs, cushions, and textiles in neutral tones, as well as modern pottery and glassware. Each piece reflects Morocco's artisanal heritage, but with a sleek, modern feel that fits effortlessly into any home.

**Location**: Avenue Al Mansour Eddahbi, Gueliz.

3. Lalla Boutique

Known for its luxurious handbags and accessories, **Lalla Boutique** offers a sophisticated selection of Moroccan-made leather goods. The brand is famous for its minimalist yet elegant handbags, which are all handcrafted in Morocco using high-quality materials. Lalla has gained a loyal following both locally and internationally for its understated luxury and timeless designs.

**What to Find**: Lalla's collection includes chic leather handbags, clutches, and tote bags in a range of colors and sizes. The designs blend traditional Moroccan leatherwork with modern, minimalist aesthetics, making them perfect for both casual and formal wear.

**Location**: Rue de la Liberté, Gueliz.

4. Max & Jan

For a blend of contemporary fashion and traditional Moroccan style, **Max & Jan** is a must-visit. This concept store, located near the Medina, offers a diverse range of clothing, accessories, and home goods. With a focus on sustainability and fair trade, Max & Jan promotes Moroccan artisans and designers who create stylish yet eco-friendly products.

**What to Find**: The boutique offers a mix of casual and chic clothing, including modern takes on traditional

Moroccan garments like kaftans and djellabas. You'll also find a selection of handmade jewelry, bags, and artisanal home décor, as well as a rooftop café where you can relax after shopping.

**Location**: 14 Rue Amsefah Sidi Abdelaziz, Medina (near the edge of Gueliz).

5. Atelier Moro

**Atelier Moro** is a design-forward boutique that specializes in handwoven textiles, ceramics, and home furnishings. The shop is known for its modern reinterpretation of traditional Moroccan craftsmanship, offering products that blend minimalist design with artisanal quality.

**What to Find**: Expect to find contemporary takes on Moroccan rugs, pillows, and throws, as well as ceramics, lamps, and decorative items. The boutique also carries limited-edition collaborations with local artisans, making it a great spot for finding unique pieces.

**Location**: Rue du Liban, Gueliz.

6. Sidi Ghanem

For those looking to explore Marrakech's design scene more thoroughly, the **Sidi Ghanem** industrial district is home to a range of workshops, showrooms, and concept stores that showcase the best of Moroccan craftsmanship and design. Located just outside the city center, Sidi Ghanem has become a hub for Moroccan artisans, furniture makers, and designers who work in a variety of mediums, from textiles to ceramics to metalwork.

**What to Find**: Sidi Ghanem is known for its high-quality home décor, custom furniture, and interior design pieces. Many of the workshops allow visitors to see artisans at work, offering a behind-the-scenes look at the making of everything from handwoven rugs to custom lighting fixtures. Popular stores include **Aït Manos** (for zellige tiles) and **KIF KIF** (for modern Moroccan furniture).

**Location**: Sidi Ghanem, just outside Marrakech.

7. Norya Ayron

If you're searching for a unique, high-fashion take on Moroccan design, **Norya Ayron** is a boutique that focuses on luxurious, handcrafted garments with a modern, bohemian flair. Known for its flowing kaftans and elegant dresses, Norya Ayron is a favorite among fashion-forward travelers.

**What to Find**: The boutique's collection includes a range of elegant kaftans, tunics, and dresses made from luxurious fabrics like silk and velvet. Norya Ayron's designs are characterized by their effortless elegance and attention to detail, making them perfect for special occasions or as stylish everyday wear.

**Location**: Rue Mouassine, Medina (close to Gueliz).

8. Lotus Privilège

Tucked away in a lush garden, **Lotus Privilège** is more than just a boutique—it's a fashion experience. The shop offers a curated selection of high-end Moroccan fashion, accessories, and home décor, blending modern luxury with traditional craftsmanship.

**What to Find**: Lotus Privilège is known for its luxurious kaftans, capes, and gowns, as well as unique jewelry and accessories crafted by Moroccan artisans. The boutique's collection is perfect for those seeking something elegant and uniquely Moroccan.

**Location**: Rue Abou Abbas El Sebti, Hivernage.

9. Place Vendôme

For lovers of high-end fashion and international luxury brands, **Place Vendôme** in Gueliz is a shopping destination not to be missed. This upscale boutique offers a selection of designer clothing, shoes, handbags, and accessories from some of the world's most famous brands.

**What to Find**: The boutique carries luxury brands such as **Chanel**, **Gucci**, and **Louis Vuitton**, making it the go-to spot for those seeking premium fashion. In addition to clothing, Place Vendôme also offers an array of high-end accessories and leather goods.

**Location**: Avenue Mohammed V, Gueliz.

10. Yves Saint Laurent Museum Boutique

For those who want to bring home a piece of the iconic fashion designer's legacy, the **Yves Saint Laurent Museum Boutique** offers a selection of elegant and exclusive items inspired by the designer's connection to Marrakech. Located next to the Jardin Majorelle, the boutique is a must-visit for fashion lovers.

**What to Find**: The boutique offers a range of high-end fashion accessories, books, and home décor items, many of which are inspired by Yves Saint Laurent's Moroccan collections. You'll also find prints and textiles that reflect the vibrant colors and patterns of the designer's work.

**Location**: Rue Yves Saint Laurent, Gueliz.

Shopping Tips

**Know Your Budget**: Marrakech's modern boutiques range from affordable to high-end luxury, so it's important to know your budget before shopping. While some concept stores focus on unique, handcrafted items that are reasonably priced, others cater to high-end shoppers seeking premium fashion and design.

**Bargaining**: Unlike in the souks, where bargaining is expected, most modern boutiques and designer stores have fixed prices. However, it's always worth asking if there are any current promotions or discounts available.

**Shipping Options**: If you're buying larger items, such as furniture or rugs, many stores offer shipping services to countries around the world. Be sure to ask about shipping costs and delivery times before making a purchase.

# Day Trips and Excursions

# Atlas Mountains: Hiking and Outdoor Adventures

**Contemporary Art and Fashion in Marrakech**

Marrakech is not only a city of rich history and traditional crafts but also a hub for contemporary art and fashion. Over the past few decades, the city has become a vibrant center for modern creativity, blending Moroccan heritage with cutting-edge design and artistic innovation. From avant-garde art galleries to fashion houses that reimagine traditional garments, Marrakech's contemporary art and fashion scene is thriving, offering visitors a unique perspective on Morocco's evolving cultural landscape.

1. Contemporary Art in Marrakech

Marrakech's art scene has gained international attention in recent years, with a growing number of galleries and cultural spaces dedicated to showcasing contemporary Moroccan and international artists. Whether you're exploring Medina or the modern neighborhoods of Gueliz and Hivernage, you'll find a range of exhibitions that reflect Morocco's dynamic artistic expression.

**MACAAL (Museum of African Contemporary Art Al Maaden)**: One of the most significant contemporary art institutions in Marrakech is the **Museum of African Contemporary Art Al Maaden** (MACAAL). Opened in 2018, MACAAL is dedicated to showcasing African art in all its forms, from painting and sculpture to photography and multimedia installations. The museum's mission is to promote African contemporary art on the global stage, with a particular focus on Moroccan artists and the African diaspora.

**What to Expect**: MACAAL hosts rotating exhibitions that explore themes such as identity, migration, and social change. Its cutting-edge architecture and serene surroundings make it a must-visit for art enthusiasts. The museum also offers workshops, artist talks, and educational programs that engage with Marrakech's creative community.

**Location**: Sidi Youssef Ben Ali, Al Maaden.

**David Bloch Gallery**: Located in Gueliz, the **David Bloch Gallery** is a contemporary art gallery specializing in urban art, abstract painting, and conceptual works. The gallery represents a mix of Moroccan and international artists, focusing on bold, modern pieces that challenge traditional boundaries.

**What to Expect**: Visitors will find a wide range of styles, from street art and graffiti to minimalist abstract works. The gallery's exhibitions frequently change, offering a fresh look at the contemporary art scene in Marrakech.

**Location**: 8 Rue des Vieux Marrakchis, Gueliz.

**Matisse Art Gallery**: Named after the French painter **Henri Matisse**, who was inspired by Moroccan art and color, the **Matisse Art Gallery** is another key destination for contemporary art lovers. The gallery showcases a wide range of mediums, including painting, photography, and sculpture, with a focus on emerging Moroccan artists.

**What to Expect**: The gallery is known for its eclectic exhibitions that blend modern techniques with Moroccan themes, often highlighting the country's landscapes, culture, and people.

**Location**: 61 Rue Yougoslavie, Gueliz.

**Le 18**: Located in the heart of Medina, **Le 18** is an experimental cultural space that hosts contemporary art exhibitions, artist residencies, and interdisciplinary projects. The venue encourages collaboration between artists, curators, and researchers, making it a unique platform for artistic exchange.

**What to Expect**: Le 18's programming includes visual art exhibitions, film screenings, performance art, and lectures, making it one of the most dynamic cultural spaces in Marrakech. Its focus on emerging talent and innovative projects ensures that each visit offers something new and unexpected.

**Location**: Derb el Ferrane, Medina.

2. Fashion in Marrakech

Marrakech has long been a source of inspiration for global fashion icons like **Yves Saint Laurent** and **Pierre Balmain**, who were drawn to the city's rich colors, textures, and traditional craftsmanship. Today, Marrakech's fashion scene continues to evolve, blending Moroccan heritage with contemporary design. Local designers are reinterpreting traditional garments, such as the **kaftan** and **djellaba**, while international fashion houses use Marrakech as a backdrop for runway shows and collections.

**Yves Saint Laurent Museum**: One of the most iconic names associated with Marrakech is Yves Saint Laurent. The designer's love affair with the city began in the 1960s, and his influence on Moroccan fashion is undeniable. The **Yves Saint Laurent Museum**, located near the Jardin Majorelle, is dedicated to his work and legacy.

**What to Expect**: The museum showcases a permanent collection of Yves Saint Laurent's most famous designs, including pieces from his groundbreaking haute couture collections. In addition to the fashion exhibits, the museum also features temporary art and photography exhibitions, as well as a research library and café.

**Location**: Rue Yves Saint Laurent, Gueliz.

**Maison ARTC**: For a glimpse into the avant-garde side of Moroccan fashion, **Maison ARTC** is a fashion studio and boutique led by designer **Artsi Ifrach**. Known for his bold, artistic designs, Artsi Ifrach creates one-of-a-kind garments that blend traditional Moroccan textiles with modern, artistic sensibilities. His work is characterized by its use of bright colors, dramatic shapes, and intricate embroidery, making it a favorite among fashion-forward travelers.

**What to Expect**: Maison ARTC offers a mix of ready-to-wear and custom-made pieces, from flowing kaftans and gowns to avant-garde accessories. The boutique is a creative space that reflects the designer's philosophy of blending tradition with innovation.

**Location**: Various locations by appointment, Gueliz.

**Moroccan Caftan Couture**: One of the most recognizable symbols of Moroccan fashion is the **kaftan**, a long, flowing gown traditionally worn at weddings and special occasions. In recent years, Moroccan designers have taken the kaftan to new heights, creating luxurious, high-fashion versions that are celebrated on runways around the world. Many designers have boutiques in Marrakech, offering bespoke kaftans that blend traditional Moroccan craftsmanship with modern elegance.

**Where to Shop**: Boutiques such as **Maison de Kaftan** and **Fadila El Gadi** specialize in high-end kaftans and traditional Moroccan attire. These designers incorporate intricate embroidery, luxurious fabrics, and contemporary cuts, creating pieces that are perfect for formal occasions or as statement fashion items.

**Location**: Various boutiques in Gueliz and Medina.

**Kaftan Queen**: Known for its modern interpretation of the traditional Moroccan kaftan, **Kaftan Queen** offers stylish, contemporary versions of this iconic garment. The brand focuses on combining luxurious fabrics with minimalist designs, making their kaftans versatile enough to be worn casually or formally.

**What to Expect**: Kaftan Queen's designs include lightweight, flowing kaftans made from silk, cotton, and linen, often in neutral tones or subtle prints. The boutique is perfect for those looking to incorporate Moroccan fashion into their everyday wardrobe.

**Location**: Rue Yves Saint Laurent, Gueliz.

**Moroccan Accessories and Jewelry**: Marrakech is also a great place to discover contemporary takes on traditional Moroccan jewelry. Local designers are reimagining **Berber jewelry** and **filigree work**, creating bold statement pieces that mix modern aesthetics with ancient techniques. For unique, handcrafted jewelry, visit boutiques like **Lalla** or the **Norya Ayron** store, where you'll find accessories that fuse tradition with fashion-forward style.

3. Fashion Events in Marrakech

Marrakech has become a popular destination for international fashion events, attracting designers, models, and industry insiders. One of the most prominent fashion events is **Caftan**, an annual fashion show that celebrates Moroccan designers and showcases the latest trends in haute couture.

**Caftan Fashion Show**: Held every year, **Caftan** is one of the most important fashion events in Morocco. The runway show features the work of top Moroccan designers, who present their latest collections of luxurious kaftans and traditional garments. The event blends fashion, art, and culture, drawing international attention and setting the trends for Moroccan couture.

**What to Expect**: The Caftan show is a glamorous affair, with models wearing intricately designed kaftans adorned with fine embroidery, beadwork, and luxurious fabrics. The event celebrates the evolution of Moroccan fashion, from its traditional roots to its modern interpretations.

**When**: Typically held in April or May.

Exploring Contemporary Art and Fashion in Marrakech

Marrakech's contemporary art and fashion scenes offer a fascinating blend of tradition and modernity, making the city a vibrant destination for creative expression. From cutting-edge galleries to fashion boutiques that push the boundaries of Moroccan style, the city is a showcase for artists and designers who are reimagining the country's rich cultural heritage. Whether you're an art lover, a fashion enthusiast, or simply curious about the intersection of past and present, Marrakech provides endless opportunities to explore its evolving artistic landscape.

## The Agafay Desert: A Taste of the Sahara

Just a short drive from the vibrant streets of Marrakech lies the **Agafay Desert**, a rocky and rugged landscape that offers travelers a taste of the Sahara's majestic beauty without the need for a long journey to the southeastern reaches of Morocco. Though not a sandy desert like the vast **Erg Chebbi** or **Erg Chigaga**, Agafay's stony plains and rolling hills create an otherworldly atmosphere that is equally breathtaking. This semi-arid wilderness is perfect for those looking to escape the city for a day or two, offering a range of outdoor adventures and luxurious experiences under the stars.

1. What Makes Agafay Special?

While the Agafay Desert doesn't have the towering dunes typically associated with the Sahara, its unique charm lies in its stark beauty and proximity to Marrakech. The landscape is a mix of rocky outcrops, dry riverbeds, and gently rolling hills that stretch into the distance. During spring, you may even catch glimpses of wildflowers blooming across the desert floor, adding a touch of color to the otherwise muted tones of the land.

**Proximity to Marrakech**: One of the biggest advantages of visiting the Agafay Desert is its location, just 40 minutes from Marrakech by car. This makes it an ideal destination for those who want to experience desert life without venturing too far from the city. It's a perfect option for a day trip or an overnight stay, providing a quick and easy escape into nature.

**Scenic Views**: The Agafay Desert offers stunning views of the **Atlas Mountains** in the distance, especially when they're snow-capped during the winter months. The juxtaposition of the rocky desert terrain with the dramatic peaks creates a beautiful, photogenic landscape that's unlike any other.

2. Desert Activities

The Agafay Desert is not just a place to admire the views; it's also a playground for outdoor enthusiasts. Whether you're looking for a thrill or simply want to relax and soak in the desert's tranquil beauty, there are plenty of activities to choose from.

**Camel Rides**: No visit to the desert is complete without a **camel ride**, and Agafay offers the perfect setting for this quintessential Moroccan experience. You'll have the opportunity to ride through the rocky plains atop a camel, swaying gently as you take in the sweeping vistas. Camel rides can range from short, scenic routes to longer treks, making them suitable for all levels of adventure.

**Quad Biking**: For those seeking more excitement, **quad biking** is a popular activity in the Agafay Desert. Explore the rugged terrain at high speeds, navigating through rocky paths and dry riverbeds while enjoying the thrill of off-road driving. Many operators offer guided tours, ensuring that even beginners can safely enjoy the experience.

**Horseback Riding**: If you prefer a more peaceful way to explore the desert, **horseback riding** is a fantastic option. Local stables offer guided rides through the Agafay's beautiful landscapes, allowing you to connect with nature while enjoying a leisurely ride on horseback.

**Hiking**: The Agafay Desert is also a great destination for **hiking**. The wide-open spaces and rolling hills provide plenty of opportunities for exploration on foot. Whether you're embarking on a short walk or a longer trek, you'll find peace and solitude in the vast desert landscape.

**Desert Picnics and Stargazing**: For a more laid-back experience, many tour operators offer **desert picnics** or **sunset dinners** in the Agafay Desert. Enjoy traditional Moroccan cuisine in a stunning natural setting as the sun sets behind the Atlas Mountains. After dark, the desert's clear skies make for incredible **stargazing**, far away from the light pollution of the city.

3. Luxury Camps and Glamping

One of the best ways to experience the Agafay Desert is to spend the night in one of the luxurious **glamping camps** that dot the landscape. These camps offer the perfect balance between adventure and comfort, providing guests with the opportunity to enjoy the beauty of the desert without sacrificing modern amenities.

**Luxury Tents**: Most camps feature **luxury tents** that come equipped with comfortable beds, private bathrooms, and stylish interiors that blend traditional Moroccan design with modern touches. Staying in a tented camp allows you to immerse yourself in the tranquility of the desert while still enjoying the comforts of a boutique hotel.

**Dining Under the Stars**: Many of the camps offer gourmet **dining experiences**, where guests can enjoy delicious Moroccan cuisine under the stars. The combination of fine dining, a cozy campfire, and the desert's vast, open skies creates an unforgettable atmosphere.

**Agafay Desert Camp**: One of the most popular camps in the region is **Agafay Desert Camp**, known for its luxurious accommodations and excellent service. The camp offers a range of activities, including camel rides, quad biking, and yoga, making it a great option for those looking to experience the desert's natural beauty in style.

4. Day Trips and Overnight Stays

Thanks to its close proximity to Marrakech, the Agafay Desert is a popular destination for both **day trips** and **overnight stays**. Many tour operators offer packages that include transportation, activities, and meals, allowing you to experience the best of the desert with ease.

**Day Trip Itineraries**: A typical day trip to the Agafay Desert might include a camel ride or quad biking in the morning, followed by lunch at a desert camp or local restaurant. In the afternoon, you'll have time to relax or explore before returning to Marrakech in the late afternoon or evening.

**Overnight Stays**: For those who want to fully experience the magic of the desert, an overnight stay is highly recommended. Watching the sunset over the desert and waking up to the peaceful stillness of the early morning are experiences you won't forget. Most camps offer comfortable accommodations, with options ranging from basic to luxury, ensuring that there's something to suit every traveler's budget.

5. Best Time to Visit

The best time to visit the Agafay Desert is during the **spring** (March to May) or **fall** (September to

November), when temperatures are mild and pleasant. Summers can be extremely hot, making outdoor activities uncomfortable, while winters can be chilly, especially at night. However, the clear winter skies make for excellent stargazing, and the snow-capped Atlas Mountains create a stunning backdrop for desert adventures.

A Desert Escape Close to Marrakech

The Agafay Desert offers a unique opportunity to experience Morocco's wild landscapes without venturing too far from Marrakech. Whether you're seeking adventure, relaxation, or a luxurious night under the stars, this rocky desert provides the perfect escape from city life. With its stunning views, thrilling activities, and comfortable camps, the Agafay Desert is an ideal destination for travelers looking to explore the natural beauty of Morocco's deserts.

**Visiting Essaouira:** The Windy City by the Sea

Located along Morocco's Atlantic coast, the charming city of **Essaouira** offers a refreshing change of pace from the bustling energy of Marrakech. Known for its strong coastal winds, which have earned it the nickname "**The Windy City**," Essaouira has long attracted visitors with its laid-back vibe, rich history, and stunning natural beauty. Whether you're drawn to its windswept beaches, the historic **Medina**, or the vibrant arts scene, Essaouira is a coastal gem that offers something for everyone.

1. A Brief History of Essaouira

Essaouira's history dates back to ancient times, but it was in the 18th century that the city, then known as **Mogador**, became a major port under the rule of Sultan **Moulay Abdallah**. He invited European architects to design the fortified city you see today, blending Moroccan and European influences to create a harmonious urban landscape. Over the centuries, Essaouira has been a crossroads for trade, culture, and religion, and its well-preserved architecture reflects the many layers of its history.

In 2001, Essaouira's **Medina** was declared a **UNESCO World Heritage Site**, recognizing its cultural and architectural significance. Today, Essaouira retains its maritime charm, attracting visitors with its historic fortifications, bustling port, and vibrant arts scene.

2. Exploring the Medina

The **Medina of Essaouira** is a highlight of any visit, offering a maze of narrow streets lined with whitewashed buildings adorned with bright blue doors and shutters. The Medina is smaller and more relaxed than those in Marrakech or Fez, making it easy to explore without the same intensity of crowds and vendors.

**Souks and Shopping**: Essaouira's Medina is home to a variety of **souks** (markets), where you can shop for traditional Moroccan crafts, including **woodwork**, **textiles**, **jewelry**, and **pottery**. The city is particularly famous for its **Thuya wood** products, intricately carved and polished pieces made from local wood that's unique to the region. Whether you're looking for a handmade box, chess set, or furniture, the craftsmanship is impressive.

**Skala de la Ville**: The **Skala de la Ville** is one of Essaouira's most iconic landmarks. This fortified wall, complete with cannons facing the sea, was built in the 18th century to protect the city from invasions. Walking along the ramparts, you'll be treated to stunning views of the Atlantic Ocean and the city's fishing port. The Skala de la Ville is also a popular spot for photographers, thanks to its dramatic seascapes and historic architecture.

**Art and Culture**: Essaouira has long been a hub for artists and musicians, and its artistic spirit is evident throughout Medina. You'll find numerous art galleries showcasing the work of local painters, sculptors, and photographers. The **Galerie d'Art Frederic Damgaard**

and **Galerie La Kasbah** are two of the most renowned galleries, offering a mix of contemporary and traditional Moroccan art.

3. The Port and Fish Market

Essaouira's bustling **port** is one of the city's most vibrant spots and a reminder of its maritime heritage. The port is still an active fishing hub, where you can watch fishermen unload their daily catch of **sardines**, **sea bass**, and other fresh seafood. The sight of the traditional **blue fishing boats** bobbing in the water against the backdrop of the Skala fortifications is iconic.

**Fish Market**: Near the port, the **fish market** offers visitors the chance to enjoy some of the freshest seafood in Morocco. You can select your fish or seafood from the market, and local vendors will grill it for you on the spot. It's a casual but delicious way to enjoy a meal, with the flavors of the sea cooked to perfection.

4. Essaouira's Beaches

Essaouira is well known for its long, windswept beaches, which attract both sun-seekers and water sports enthusiasts. The city's strong **Alizé winds** make it one of the best places in the world for **kitesurfing** and **windsurfing**, with many surf schools offering lessons for beginners and equipment rentals for experienced surfers.

**Plage d'Essaouira**: The main beach, **Plage d'Essaouira**, stretches for miles along the coast, providing plenty of space for beachgoers to relax. While the wind can be too strong for comfortable sunbathing at times, the beach is perfect for long walks, horseback riding, or simply watching the kite surfers glide across the water.

**Sidi Kaouki**: For a more remote beach experience, head to **Sidi Kaouki**, a quieter stretch of coastline located about 25 kilometers south of Essaouira. This beach is less developed and has a more rugged feel, making it ideal for those looking to escape the crowds and enjoy a peaceful day by the sea. Sidi Kaouki is also popular with surfers and windsurfers.

5. Festivals and Music

Essaouira is known for its vibrant music scene, particularly its connection to **Gnawa music**, a traditional genre with roots in West Africa. The city hosts the annual **Essaouira Gnaoua and World Music Festival**, which draws musicians and music lovers from around the world.

**Gnawa Music**: Gnawa music is deeply spiritual, blending African, Berber, and Arabic influences. The rhythmic, trance-like sounds are created using instruments such as the **guembri** (a three-stringed bass) and **qraqeb** (metal castanets). In Essaouira, you can often hear Gnawa musicians performing in the streets or in local venues, making it a key part of the city's cultural experience.

**Gnawa and World Music Festival**: Held every summer, this festival celebrates both traditional Gnawa music and global music from a wide range of genres, including jazz, reggae, and blues. The festival takes place in the city's historic squares and beaches, turning Essaouira into a lively hub of music and culture for several days.

6. Outdoor Adventures

Beyond the beach, Essaouira offers plenty of opportunities for outdoor adventures. From hiking in the nearby **Argan tree forests** to exploring the dunes on camelback, there's something for every type of traveler.

**Argan Oil Cooperatives**: The region surrounding Essaouira is home to the **Argan tree**, which produces the fruit used to make **argan oil**—a product prized for its culinary and cosmetic uses. Many local cooperatives offer tours where you can learn about the traditional methods used to extract argan oil and purchase high-quality products directly from the source.

**Camel and Horseback Rides**: Exploring the beaches and dunes on camelback or horseback is a popular activity in Essaouira. Tours range from short rides along the beach to longer excursions that take you into the surrounding countryside, offering a unique way to experience the landscape.

7. Best Time to Visit

The best time to visit Essaouira is during the **spring** (March to May) and **fall** (September to November), when the weather is pleasant and the winds are not too strong. Summer can be windy but is also when the Gnawa and World Music Festival takes place, attracting visitors from around the world. Winter is mild, but the cooler temperatures and strong winds make beach activities less appealing.

A Coastal Haven

Essaouira's relaxed pace, artistic atmosphere, and scenic beauty make it one of Morocco's most enchanting coastal destinations. Whether you're wandering through the historic Medina, dining on freshly grilled seafood by the port, or enjoying a walk along the windswept beach, Essaouira offers a tranquil escape with a touch of adventure. Its rich cultural history, combined with the natural beauty of the Atlantic coast, makes Essaouira a must-visit for anyone exploring Morocco.

## Wellness and Relaxation

## Hammams: Experiencing Moroccan Baths

No trip to Morocco is complete without indulging in the ancient tradition of the **hammam**, a public steam bath that plays a central role in Moroccan culture. Rooted in centuries of tradition, the hammam is more than just a place for cleansing the body—it's a ritual for relaxation, rejuvenation, and social connection. Whether you visit a traditional local hammam or a luxurious spa, experiencing a Moroccan bath is a chance to unwind and immerse yourself in one of Morocco's most beloved wellness traditions.

1. What Is a Hammam?

A **hammam** is a type of steam bath or sauna where Moroccans go to cleanse their skin, relax their muscles, and unwind. The practice of visiting the hammam is deeply embedded in Moroccan life, with both men and women attending regularly—often once a week—as part of their self-care routine. Traditionally, hammams are not only for hygiene but also serve as social hubs where friends and family gather to catch up and enjoy the ritual together.

Hammams usually consist of several rooms with varying levels of heat, starting with a **warm room** to open the pores and progressing to a **hot steam room**. After spending time in the steam, bathers undergo a rigorous scrubbing, followed by rinsing, leaving the skin exfoliated, soft, and deeply cleansed.

2. Types of Hammams

When visiting Marrakech or any other Moroccan city, you'll find two main types of hammams: **traditional public hammams** and **luxury hammams** in spas and hotels. Each offers a unique experience, so whether you want to experience an authentic, local hammam or indulge in a more luxurious setting, you'll find an option that suits your preferences.

**Traditional Public Hammams**: These hammams are frequented by locals and offer an authentic Moroccan bathing experience. Public hammams are typically gender-segregated, with men and women bathing at separate times or in separate areas. You'll be provided with basic bath essentials like black soap, a scrubbing mitt (known as a **kessa**), and buckets of water for rinsing. While traditional hammams are less luxurious, they offer a chance to connect with Moroccan culture and experience the bathhouse as locals do.

**Luxury Hammams and Spas**: For those seeking a more relaxing and pampered experience, Marrakech is home to many luxury hammams located in upscale spas and hotels. These hammams combine the traditional Moroccan bathing rituals with modern comforts, offering plush surroundings, professional staff, and additional treatments like massages, facials, and aromatherapy. In these settings, the experience is designed to be deeply rejuvenating, with luxurious touches like high-quality oils, soft towels, and calming music.

3. The Hammam Ritual

Whether you're visiting a local hammam or a luxury spa, the hammam ritual follows a similar process, involving several stages that are designed to cleanse and relax both the body and mind.

**Stage 1: Warming Up**
Upon entering the hammam, you'll be led into a warm, humid room, where the heat helps to open your pores and soften your skin. You'll be given a bucket of warm

water to pour over yourself, allowing your body to adjust to the heat while relaxing your muscles.

## Stage 2: Black Soap Application
After warming up, you'll apply **savon noir** (black soap) to your skin. This traditional Moroccan soap is made from olive oil and crushed olives, and it has a smooth, creamy texture. The soap is left on the skin for several minutes, helping to soften it further and prepare it for exfoliation.

## Stage 3: Exfoliation
The next stage is the most important: exfoliation. Using a **kessa** glove, either a hammam attendant or yourself will scrub your skin rigorously to remove dead skin cells and impurities. This process may feel intense, especially in traditional hammams, but it leaves the skin incredibly smooth and rejuvenated. The scrub is typically followed by a thorough rinse with warm water.

## Stage 4: Ghassoul Clay Mask (Optional)
In some hammams, particularly luxury spas, a **ghassoul clay mask** may be applied after exfoliation. Ghassoul is a mineral-rich clay found in the Atlas Mountains and is known for its purifying and skin-softening properties. The clay is applied to the body and sometimes the hair, and after it dries, it's rinsed off, leaving the skin feeling fresh and revitalized.

**Stage 5: Relaxation and Hydration**
After the cleansing process, you'll move to a cooler room to relax. Many hammams offer herbal teas or water to help you rehydrate. In luxury hammams, this stage often includes additional treatments like a soothing massage, further enhancing the relaxation experience.

4. Hammam Etiquette

When visiting a hammam, especially a traditional public one, it's important to be aware of certain customs and etiquette to ensure a respectful and enjoyable experience.

**What to Wear**: In traditional hammams, bathers typically wear minimal clothing, such as underwear or a bathing suit bottom, as full nudity is not common. In luxury hammams, you'll often be provided with disposable underwear or a robe. It's always a good idea to bring your own towel and flip-flops for hygiene purposes.

**Bring Your Own Essentials**: While luxury hammams provide everything you need, traditional hammams may require you to bring your own **black soap**, **kessa**, shampoo, and other personal hygiene items. Many local shops around the hammam sell these essentials, so it's easy to purchase them before you enter.

**Gender Segregation**: Hammams in Morocco are generally gender-segregated, with separate areas or different times for men and women. If you're visiting with a partner of the opposite sex, you'll need to go in separately.

**Respect Local Customs**: While hammams are social spaces, particularly for women, it's important to maintain a respectful tone and behavior. Conversations tend to be low-key, and modesty is observed, even in such relaxed settings.

5. Best Hammams in Marrakech

Marrakech is home to a wide variety of hammams, from humble neighborhood bathhouses to opulent spa retreats. Here are some of the best options for both traditional and luxury hammam experiences:

**Hammam Mouassine**: One of the oldest hammams in Marrakech, **Hammam Mouassine** is a traditional bathhouse located in the Medina. It offers an authentic, no-frills experience where you can scrub, steam, and cleanse like a local. The historic architecture and affordable prices make it a popular choice for travelers seeking an authentic hammam experience.

**Les Bains de Marrakech**: A luxurious hammam and spa located near the Kasbah, **Les Bains de Marrakech**

offers a high-end experience with beautifully designed steam rooms, professional therapists, and a wide range of treatments. It's perfect for those looking to relax in style and enjoy additional treatments like massages and facials.

**Hammam de la Rose**: Located in the heart of the Medina, **Hammam de la Rose** is a beautifully designed spa that blends tradition with luxury. The hammam experience here is soothing and rejuvenating, with a focus on relaxation and high-quality service. It's a popular choice for visitors looking for a more refined hammam experience.

**Royal Mansour Spa**: For the ultimate indulgence, the **Royal Mansour Spa** offers one of the most luxurious hammam experiences in Marrakech. The opulent surroundings, personalized treatments, and exceptional service make it a standout choice for those seeking the highest level of pampering.

6. Benefits of the Hammam

The hammam ritual is not just a cleansing process; it also offers a range of health and wellness benefits:

**Exfoliation and Skin Health**: The intense scrubbing removes dead skin cells, unclogs pores, and improves circulation, leaving the skin smooth, soft, and rejuvenated.

**Detoxification**: The steam helps to open pores and flush out toxins from the body, promoting overall health and well-being.

**Relaxation**: The combination of heat, steam, and scrubbing relaxes muscles, eases tension, and promotes deep relaxation, making it an excellent way to unwind after a busy day of sightseeing.

A Hammam Experience to Remember

Experiencing a Moroccan hammam is a must for anyone visiting Marrakech. Whether you choose a traditional public bathhouse for an authentic, down-to-earth experience or opt for the luxury of a spa hammam, the ritual of cleansing, exfoliating, and relaxing in a hammam is deeply rejuvenating. It's a timeless tradition that allows you to connect with Moroccan culture while also indulging in the ultimate form of wellness and relaxation.

## Spa and Wellness Retreats: Indulging in Luxury and Rejuvenation

Marrakech is not only known for its vibrant souks and stunning architecture but also for its world-class **spa and wellness retreats**. Whether you're looking to unwind after a day of exploring or embark on a holistic wellness journey, Marrakech offers an array of luxurious spas and wellness centers that cater to both physical and mental relaxation. From traditional Moroccan hammam rituals to modern spa treatments, these retreats combine ancient practices with contemporary comforts, making them a haven for wellness enthusiasts.

1. The Spa at Royal Mansour

For the ultimate in luxury, the **Royal Mansour Spa** is one of Marrakech's most prestigious wellness retreats. Located within the lavish Royal Mansour Hotel, the spa is an architectural masterpiece that offers a serene escape from the bustling city. Its intricate design features white latticework, marble floors, and lush gardens, creating an atmosphere of calm and opulence.

**What to Expect**: The Royal Mansour Spa offers a wide range of treatments, including traditional **hammam rituals**, **massages**, **facials**, and **beauty therapies**. The spa's wellness programs are designed to promote relaxation, rejuvenation, and holistic healing, with treatments incorporating high-end products and natural Moroccan ingredients like **argan oil** and **rosewater**. The spa also features a stunning **indoor swimming pool**, private relaxation areas, and a tearoom where guests can unwind after their treatments.

**Signature Treatments**: The **Royal Hammam Ritual** is a must-try, offering a luxurious twist on the traditional Moroccan bath experience. The treatment includes a black soap scrub, steam bath, and body wrap using **ghassoul clay**, followed by a soothing massage.

**Location**: Rue Abou Abbas El Sebti, Medina.

2. Les Bains de Marrakech

A favorite among visitors and locals alike, **Les Bains de Marrakech** is one of the city's most popular spas, known for its blend of traditional Moroccan treatments and luxurious facilities. Tucked away near the Kasbah, the spa offers an oasis of tranquility with its beautiful tiled rooms, candlelit ambiance, and attentive staff.

**What to Expect**: Les Bains de Marrakech offers a range of **hammam rituals**, **massages**, and **body treatments**. The spa uses high-quality natural products, including **eucalyptus**, **black soap**, and **ghassoul clay**, to ensure that every treatment is both relaxing and effective.

Guests can also enjoy the spa's heated indoor pool and soothing steam rooms.

**Signature Treatments**: The **Oriental Massage** and the **Moroccan Hammam** are highly recommended for those looking to relax and experience traditional Moroccan wellness practices. The spa also offers **couple's treatments**, making it a great choice for a romantic retreat.

**Location**: Rue Riad Zitoun el Jdid, Medina.

3. La Sultana Spa

Located in the heart of the **Kasbah district**, the **La Sultana Spa** is part of the luxurious La Sultana Hotel, known for its opulent design and intimate atmosphere. The spa offers an immersive wellness experience that combines ancient Moroccan traditions with modern spa treatments, all set in a stunning setting of arches, carved stone, and lush greenery.

**What to Expect**: The La Sultana Spa features a range of traditional hammam rituals, aromatherapy massages, and beauty treatments. The spa's serene environment, complete with marble baths, candlelit relaxation rooms, and a heated pool, creates the perfect setting for relaxation. Guests can also enjoy **yoga sessions** and **meditation** classes, making it a holistic wellness retreat.

**Signature Treatments**: The **Sultana Hammam** is a luxurious treatment that includes a black soap scrub, steam bath, and massage with argan oil. The spa's **anti-stress massage** is also a popular choice for those looking to unwind after a long day of sightseeing.

**Location**: Rue de la Kasbah, Medina.

4. Es Saadi Palace Spa

The **Es Saadi Palace Spa** is an expansive wellness retreat located within the **Es Saadi Palace**, offering a wide range of treatments designed to promote both relaxation and rejuvenation. The spa is set within lush gardens and features state-of-the-art facilities, including a **hydrotherapy pool**, **saunas**, **steam rooms**, and **treatment cabins**.

**What to Expect**: Es Saadi Palace Spa offers traditional Moroccan treatments, including hammams, scrubs, and massages, as well as modern beauty therapies like anti-aging facials and detox programs. The spa uses natural ingredients, including argan oil and essential oils, to nourish and heal the skin. Guests can also enjoy yoga and meditation classes as part of the wellness experience.

**Signature Treatments**: The **Essentiel Detox Ritual** is a complete wellness journey, including a detoxifying hammam session, a full-body exfoliation, and a nourishing body wrap using ghassoul clay and essential oils. The spa's **anti-aging treatments** are also popular for their rejuvenating effects.

**Location**: Rue Ibrahim El Mazini, Hivernage.

5. Le Spa at Mandarin Oriental

For a modern and holistic approach to wellness, the **Le Spa at Mandarin Oriental** offers a world-class spa experience surrounded by beautiful gardens and views of the Atlas Mountains. The spa focuses on **holistic healing** and **mind-body wellness**, blending traditional Moroccan rituals with Asian-inspired therapies to create a peaceful and luxurious retreat.

**What to Expect**: The spa features private hammams, indoor and outdoor pools, steam rooms, and relaxation areas, offering a wide range of treatments including massages, body scrubs, and facials. The spa's holistic approach incorporates **aromatherapy**, **meditation**, and **yoga**, making it a comprehensive wellness retreat for those seeking relaxation and rejuvenation.

**Signature Treatments**: The **Oriental Wellness Ritual** is a signature treatment that includes a full-body massage with essential oils, followed by a detoxifying scrub and relaxing steam session. The spa also offers **personalized**

**wellness programs**, including detox retreats and stress-relief treatments.

**Location**: Route du Golf Royal, Marrakech.

6. The Pearl Spa

Located in the chic **Hivernage district**, the **Pearl Spa** at the Pearl Marrakech hotel is a sleek and modern spa offering a range of luxurious treatments designed for ultimate relaxation. The spa features a stunning indoor pool, a well-equipped gym, and beautifully designed treatment rooms, making it a favorite among travelers looking for a stylish wellness retreat.

**What to Expect**: The Pearl Spa offers everything from traditional hammam experiences to advanced facial treatments and relaxing massages. The spa uses premium products, including **La Mer** skincare, to ensure a high-end experience. Guests can also enjoy the spa's **outdoor terrace** for sunbathing or relaxation after treatments.

**Signature Treatments**: The **Pearl Hammam Experience** is a luxurious version of the traditional Moroccan bath, including a black soap scrub, clay mask, and full-body massage. The spa also offers **La Mer facials** for those seeking anti-aging and hydrating skin treatments.

**Location**: Avenue Echouhada, Hivernage.

7. Selman Marrakech Spa

Set within the glamorous **Selman Marrakech Hotel**, the **Selman Spa** offers a unique wellness experience that blends traditional Moroccan treatments with equestrian-inspired therapies. The hotel's world-renowned Arabian horses play a role in the wellness offerings, with **equitherapy** sessions available for guests seeking a more holistic connection with nature.

**What to Expect**: The Selman Spa features private hammam rooms, a hydrotherapy pool, and beautifully designed treatment rooms that reflect the luxurious style of the hotel. The spa offers a range of massages, body treatments, and beauty therapies, all designed to promote relaxation and balance.

**Signature Treatments**: The **Selman Signature Massage** is a deeply relaxing treatment that uses warm oils and gentle techniques to ease tension and restore balance. The spa's **equestrian wellness programs** are also unique, offering guests the chance to connect with horses through therapeutic activities.

**Location**: Route d'Amizmiz, Marrakech.

8. Wellness Programs and Retreats

Many of Marrakech's top spas offer more than just individual treatments—they also provide **wellness retreats** and programs designed to promote long-term health and well-being. Whether you're looking to detox, de-stress, or focus on fitness, these retreats often include personalized treatments, yoga and meditation sessions, and healthy meals, allowing guests to immerse themselves in a holistic wellness experience.

**Detox Retreats**: For those looking to cleanse and rejuvenate, several spas in Marrakech offer detox programs that include cleansing diets, detoxifying body treatments, and holistic therapies aimed at eliminating toxins and restoring balance to the body.

**Yoga and Meditation Retreats**: Yoga enthusiasts will find a variety of retreats focused on deepening their practice and enhancing mental clarity. These retreats often combine daily yoga sessions with mindfulness practices and spa treatments, creating a comprehensive wellness experience.

The Ultimate Wellness Escape

Marrakech's spa and wellness retreats offer a luxurious escape for travelers seeking relaxation, rejuvenation, and holistic healing. Whether you're indulging in a traditional hammam, enjoying a massage with views of the Atlas Mountains, or embarking on a wellness retreat, the city's spas provide a blend of ancient rituals and modern therapies. No matter which spa you choose, you're sure to leave Marrakech feeling refreshed, revitalized, and deeply relaxed.

# Staying in Marrakech

## Riads vs. Hotels: Where to Stay

One of the most important decisions when planning your trip to Marrakech is choosing the perfect accommodation. The city offers a wide variety of lodging options, but two types stand out: **riads** and **hotels**. Each offers a distinct experience, and deciding between them will depend on your personal preferences, travel style, and the kind of atmosphere you're looking for. This chapter explores the differences between riads and hotels to help you decide where to stay in Marrakech.

1. What Is a Riad?

A **riad** is a traditional Moroccan house or palace with a central courtyard or garden. The word "riad" comes from the Arabic word for "garden," and this design reflects a focus on creating an inward-facing sanctuary, providing peace and privacy from the busy streets outside. Many riads are located in the **Medina**, the historic part of the city, and have been beautifully restored and converted into boutique guesthouses.

**Architectural Features**: Riads are known for their traditional Moroccan architecture, including **zellige tilework**, **carved woodwork**, and intricate **plaster**

**decorations**. The central courtyard, often featuring a fountain or small pool, serves as a peaceful retreat for guests to relax and escape the hustle and bustle of the city. Many riads also have **rooftop terraces**, offering stunning views of the Medina and the distant Atlas Mountains.

**Personalized Service**: One of the main attractions of staying in a riad is the intimate and personalized experience. Riads are typically smaller than hotels, often with only a handful of rooms, allowing for a more tailored guest experience. Many riads are family-owned, and the hosts often go above and beyond to make guests feel welcome, offering home-cooked breakfasts, personalized recommendations, and a warm, friendly atmosphere.

**Cultural Immersion**: Staying in a riad allows you to experience Morocco's rich culture and heritage firsthand. The traditional decor, the layout, and even the meals are designed to reflect Moroccan customs and hospitality. For travelers looking to immerse themselves in the local culture, a riad offers an authentic experience.

2. What Is a Hotel?

While riads offer a traditional Moroccan experience, **hotels** in Marrakech range from luxurious international chains to modern boutique properties. Hotels can be found both in the heart of Medina and in the more modern neighborhoods of **Gueliz** and **Hivernage**, offering a different kind of stay with more standardized amenities and services.

**Range of Amenities**: Hotels often provide a wider range of amenities compared to riads, including **swimming pools**, **fitness centers**, **spas**, **restaurants**, and sometimes even nightclubs or bars. For travelers seeking a more resort-like experience, complete with modern conveniences, hotels may be the better option. Many luxury hotels in Marrakech, such as the **Four Seasons**, **Mandarin Oriental**, and **La Mamounia**, offer world-class facilities, including expansive pools, high-end spas, and gourmet dining.

**Larger Capacity**: Hotels generally have more rooms than riads, making them ideal for larger groups, families, or business travelers. The staff in hotels are usually trained to cater to a diverse range of guests, ensuring a high level of professionalism and service. However, this can sometimes mean a less personal experience compared to staying in a riad.

**Modern Design**: While many hotels incorporate Moroccan design elements, they also offer modern, international-style decor and layouts. Rooms are typically larger, with contemporary furnishings and high-tech amenities like **flat-screen TVs**, **Wi-Fi**, and **air**

**conditioning**. For travelers who prefer a more cosmopolitan feel or need certain comforts, hotels can provide these with ease.

3. The Benefits of Staying in a Riad

For travelers seeking a more intimate, culturally rich experience, staying in a riad offers several unique benefits:

**Authenticity and Charm**: The charm of a riad lies in its authentic Moroccan architecture, decor, and atmosphere. Each riad is unique, offering a personalized experience that transports you into the heart of Moroccan history and culture. Many guests appreciate the peaceful retreat a riad provides after a day of exploring the lively streets of the Medina.

**Proximity to the Medina**: Most riads are located within the Medina, meaning you're just steps away from Marrakech's famous souks, historical sites, and bustling squares like **Jemaa el-Fnaa**. Staying in a riad allows you to fully experience the rhythm of the Medina, with easy access to its narrow alleyways, markets, and restaurants.

**Quiet and Relaxing Ambiance**: Despite being in the heart of the city, riads offer a quiet and serene environment. The inward-facing design blocks out the noise of the streets, creating a tranquil space for relaxation. The central courtyards, often filled with plants and the sound of running water, add to the peaceful ambiance.

**Personal Touch**: The small size and intimate nature of riads mean that the service is often more personalized. Many riads offer traditional Moroccan meals made from fresh, local ingredients, and some even provide cooking classes or other cultural experiences. The hosts are often more involved in making sure you have a memorable stay.

4. The Benefits of Staying in a Hotel

Hotels, especially luxury and boutique options, come with their own set of advantages, making them an attractive choice for travelers who prioritize convenience, amenities, and a modern feel:

**Full-Service Amenities**: Hotels often have a range of facilities, including pools, spas, gyms, and restaurants, giving guests everything they need for a comfortable and relaxing stay. For those who want to indulge in **luxury spa treatments**, enjoy **fine dining**, or simply relax by a large pool, hotels can provide these conveniences all in one place.

**Modern Comforts**: Hotels tend to offer more modern amenities, such as **room service**, **business centers**, and state-of-the-art technology. If you're traveling for business or simply prefer a more contemporary style, hotels are better suited to provide these comforts.

**Consistent Service**: Hotels are known for their consistency in service and quality. With international standards, many luxury hotels in Marrakech offer the kind of reliability and professionalism that international travelers expect. Whether it's housekeeping, concierge services, or on-site dining, hotels tend to be more predictable in their offerings.

**Variety of Locations**: While many riads are concentrated in the Medina, hotels can be found throughout the city, including in the modern districts of Gueliz and Hivernage. These areas offer a more cosmopolitan experience, with wide boulevards, upscale restaurants, and shopping malls, providing a different perspective on Marrakech.

5. Which Is Right for You?

The choice between staying in a riad or a hotel comes down to your personal travel style and the type of experience you want to have in Marrakech.

**Choose a Riad If You Want**:

An authentic and immersive Moroccan experience.

To stay in a traditional setting with cultural charm.

Personalized service and a quieter, more intimate atmosphere.

To be close to the Medina and its attractions.

**Choose a Hotel If You Want**:

Modern amenities and conveniences, such as pools, spas, and gyms.

A larger space with consistent, high-quality service.

Access to on-site restaurants, bars, and international dining options.

A more cosmopolitan stay in districts like Gueliz or Hivernage.

6. Top Recommendations

Here are a few of the top riads and hotels in Marrakech, known for their exceptional service and unique atmosphere:

**Top Riads**:

**Riad El Fenn**: A chic, boutique riad with luxurious rooms, a rooftop terrace, and a stylish blend of modern and traditional decor.

**Riad Kniza**: A beautifully restored 18th-century riad known for its authentic Moroccan atmosphere, personalized service, and traditional cuisine.

**Riad Yasmine**: Famous for its Instagram-worthy courtyard and pool, Riad Yasmine offers a serene and trendy escape in the heart of the Medina.

**Top Hotels**:

**La Mamounia**: A world-renowned luxury hotel offering opulent rooms, a lavish spa, and stunning gardens, often regarded as one of the best hotels in the world.

**Four Seasons Resort Marrakech**: A modern, family-friendly resort with large pools, excellent dining options, and beautiful views of the Atlas Mountains.

**Es Saadi Palace**: A luxury hotel and spa located in the Hivernage district, offering a mix of Moroccan charm and modern amenities, including a casino and several restaurants.

Finding Your Perfect Stay

Whether you choose a traditional riad or a modern hotel, both options offer something special in Marrakech. Riads provide a unique, intimate experience steeped in

Moroccan culture, while hotels offer modern comforts and a wide range of amenities. No matter where you stay, Marrakech's hospitality will ensure that your visit is unforgettable.

## Best Budget, Mid-range, and Luxury Accommodations

Marrakech offers a wide variety of accommodations to suit every budget and style, from affordable options for budget-conscious travelers to opulent hotels for those seeking a luxurious escape. Whether you're looking for a charming riad in the heart of the Medina, a modern boutique hotel in the city's trendy neighborhoods, or a five-star resort with all the amenities, Marrakech has something for everyone. In this section, we'll highlight the best options in each category to help you find the perfect place to stay during your visit.

1. Best Budget Accommodations

For travelers on a budget, Marrakech offers a range of affordable riads and guesthouses that provide comfort, charm, and an authentic Moroccan experience without breaking the bank. These options often include breakfast, and while they may be more basic, they still deliver excellent service and a taste of Moroccan hospitality.

### Riad Boussa

Located in the heart of Medina, **Riad Boussa** is a cozy and affordable riad offering excellent value for money. With just a few rooms, the riad provides personalized service in a peaceful setting. The rooms are simply furnished but comfortable, and the rooftop terrace is perfect for relaxing after a day of exploring the city. Guests love the friendly hosts and the homemade breakfasts served daily.

**Price Range**: $60–$80 per night

**Location**: Medina

### Riad Dar Thalge

**Riad Dar Thalge** is a budget-friendly option located in a quieter area of the Medina, offering easy access to the city's main attractions. The riad features a small central courtyard, a rooftop terrace, and traditionally decorated rooms with private bathrooms. The owners are known for their warm hospitality and helpfulness in organizing excursions and activities for guests.

**Price Range**: $50–$75 per night

**Location**: Medina

**Equity Point Marrakech**

For backpackers and budget travelers, **Equity Point Marrakech** is a popular hostel located in a former palace in Medina. The hostel offers dormitory-style rooms and private rooms, as well as a pool, rooftop terrace, and on-site restaurant. It's a great place for social travelers to meet others and enjoy an affordable stay with a central location.

**Price Range**: $20–$50 per night

**Location**: Medina

2. Best Mid-range Accommodations

If you're looking for a balance between comfort, style, and affordability, Marrakech's mid-range accommodations provide excellent value. These riads and boutique hotels often feature beautiful Moroccan design, a range of amenities, and personalized service, making them ideal for travelers who want more comfort without splurging on luxury.

**Riad Jona**

**Riad Jona** is a charming mid-range riad located just a short walk from Jemaa el-Fnaa square. The riad offers well-decorated rooms, a rooftop terrace with a plunge pool, and a spa with traditional hammam treatments. Guests can enjoy a daily breakfast, and the on-site restaurant serves delicious Moroccan cuisine. The friendly staff and comfortable atmosphere make it a top choice for travelers looking for quality at a reasonable price.

**Price Range**: $100–$150 per night

**Location**: Medina

**2Ciels Boutique Hotel & Spa**
Located in the modern Gueliz district, **2Ciels Boutique Hotel & Spa** offers a contemporary and stylish stay with mid-range prices. The hotel features spacious, modern rooms with Moroccan-inspired decor, a rooftop pool with stunning views of the city, and a full-service spa. Guests appreciate the hotel's central location near restaurants, shops, and cafes, as well as the rooftop restaurant and bar.

**Price Range**: $120–$180 per night

**Location**: Gueliz

**Riad Yasmine**
Known for its Instagram-worthy courtyard and pool, **Riad Yasmine** is a mid-range gem in the Medina. The riad features beautifully designed rooms with traditional Moroccan decor, a central courtyard with a small pool, and a rooftop terrace with panoramic views of the city. It's the perfect place to unwind after exploring the

bustling streets of the Medina, and the warm hospitality of the staff ensures a memorable stay.

**Price Range**: $120–$160 per night

**Location**: Medina

3. Best Luxury Accommodations

Marrakech is home to some of the most luxurious hotels and riads in the world, offering opulent surroundings, world-class service, and an unforgettable experience. Whether you want to stay in a palatial riad, a five-star resort, or a high-end boutique hotel, these luxury accommodations will ensure a stay filled with indulgence and comfort.

**La Mamounia**
One of Marrakech's most iconic hotels, **La Mamounia** is the epitome of luxury and elegance. Set within lush gardens just outside the Medina, this five-star hotel has been a favorite of celebrities and royalty for decades. The hotel features lavishly decorated rooms and suites, a stunning spa with a traditional hammam, multiple gourmet restaurants, and expansive pools. Its blend of Moroccan design and Art Deco elements, along with impeccable service, makes it one of the most sought-after luxury stays in Marrakech.

**Price Range**: $600–$1,500 per night

**Location**: Medina (near Jemaa el-Fnaa)

**Royal Mansour**

Commissioned by the King of Morocco, **Royal Mansour** is an ultra-luxurious hotel that offers an unparalleled experience in Marrakech. The property consists of private riads, each with its own courtyard, plunge pool, and butler service. Guests can enjoy the hotel's world-class spa, fine dining restaurants, and beautifully landscaped gardens. Royal Mansour is perfect for travelers looking for ultimate privacy, exclusivity, and indulgence.

**Price Range**: $1,000–$3,000 per night

**Location**: Medina

**Amanjena**

Part of the Aman Resorts collection, **Amanjena** is a peaceful luxury retreat located just outside Marrakech, near the Atlas Mountains. The resort features spacious **pavilions** and **villas** with private pools, surrounded by beautiful gardens and reflecting pools. Guests can enjoy a full range of wellness treatments at the Aman Spa, as well as fine dining at the resort's restaurants. Amanjena is ideal for those seeking luxury and tranquility away from the city center.

**Price Range**: $800–$2,500 per night

**Location**: Outskirts of Marrakech

4. Other Noteworthy Accommodations

**Les Deux Tours**: A luxury boutique hotel set in a tranquil garden, offering private suites and villas with a blend of traditional and modern design.

**Price Range**: $250–$500 per night

**Location**: Palmeraie district

**El Fenn**: A boutique riad known for its chic decor, rooftop pool, and artistic atmosphere. It offers a luxurious stay with a focus on design and comfort.

**Price Range**: $300–$600 per night

**Location**: Medina

**Selman Marrakech**: A luxury hotel and equestrian estate that offers an extraordinary blend of Moroccan craftsmanship and opulent design.

**Price Range**: $600–$1,200 per night

**Location**: Route d'Amizmiz, Marrakech outskirts

---

A Stay for Every Style and Budget

Whether you're traveling on a budget, seeking mid-range comfort, or indulging in five-star luxury, Marrakech offers a diverse range of accommodations to suit every traveler. From traditional riads that immerse you in Moroccan culture to modern hotels with all the conveniences, the city provides endless options for a memorable stay. No matter where you choose to rest your head, Marrakech's legendary hospitality will ensure a warm welcome and a wonderful experience.

## Best Budget, Mid-range, and Luxury Accommodations

Marrakech offers a wide variety of accommodations to suit every budget and style, from affordable options for budget-conscious travelers to opulent hotels for those seeking a luxurious escape. Whether you're looking for a charming riad in the heart of the Medina, a modern boutique hotel in the city's trendy neighborhoods, or a five-star resort with all the amenities, Marrakech has something for everyone. In this section, we'll highlight the best options in each category to help you find the perfect place to stay during your visit.

1. Best Budget Accommodations

For travelers on a budget, Marrakech offers a range of affordable riads and guesthouses that provide comfort, charm, and an authentic Moroccan experience without breaking the bank. These options often include breakfast, and while they may be more basic, they still deliver excellent service and a taste of Moroccan hospitality.

**Riad Boussa**

Located in the heart of the Medina, **Riad Boussa** is a cozy and affordable riad offering excellent value for money. With just a few rooms, the riad provides personalized service in a peaceful setting. The rooms are simply furnished but comfortable, and the rooftop terrace is perfect for relaxing after a day of exploring the city. Guests love the friendly hosts and the homemade breakfasts served daily.

**Price Range**: $60–$80 per night

**Location**: Medina

**Riad Dar Thalge**

**Riad Dar Thalge** is a budget-friendly option located in a quieter area of the Medina, offering easy access to the city's main attractions. The riad features a small central courtyard, a rooftop terrace, and traditionally decorated rooms with private bathrooms. The owners are known for their warm hospitality and helpfulness in organizing excursions and activities for guests.

**Price Range**: $50–$75 per night

**Location**: Medina

**Equity Point Marrakech**
For backpackers and budget travelers, **Equity Point Marrakech** is a popular hostel located in a former palace in Medina. The hostel offers dormitory-style rooms and private rooms, as well as a pool, rooftop terrace, and on-site restaurant. It's a great place for social travelers to meet others and enjoy an affordable stay with a central location.

**Price Range**: $20–$50 per night

**Location**: Medina

2. Best Mid-range Accommodations

If you're looking for a balance between comfort, style, and affordability, Marrakech's mid-range accommodations provide excellent value. These riads and boutique hotels often feature beautiful Moroccan design, a range of amenities, and personalized service, making them ideal for travelers who want more comfort without splurging on luxury.

**Riad Jona**
**Riad Jona** is a charming mid-range riad located just a short walk from Jemaa el-Fnaa square. The riad offers

well-decorated rooms, a rooftop terrace with a plunge pool, and a spa with traditional hammam treatments. Guests can enjoy a daily breakfast, and the on-site restaurant serves delicious Moroccan cuisine. The friendly staff and comfortable atmosphere make it a top choice for travelers looking for quality at a reasonable price.

**Price Range**: $100–$150 per night

**Location**: Medina

**2Ciels Boutique Hotel & Spa**
Located in the modern Gueliz district, **2Ciels Boutique Hotel & Spa** offers a contemporary and stylish stay with mid-range prices. The hotel features spacious, modern rooms with Moroccan-inspired decor, a rooftop pool with stunning views of the city, and a full-service spa. Guests appreciate the hotel's central location near restaurants, shops, and cafes, as well as the rooftop restaurant and bar.

**Price Range**: $120–$180 per night

**Location**: Gueliz

**Riad Yasmine**
Known for its Instagram-worthy courtyard and pool, **Riad Yasmine** is a mid-range gem in the Medina. The riad features beautifully designed rooms with traditional

Moroccan decor, a central courtyard with a small pool, and a rooftop terrace with panoramic views of the city. It's the perfect place to unwind after exploring the bustling streets of the Medina, and the warm hospitality of the staff ensures a memorable stay.

**Price Range**: $120–$160 per night

**Location**: Medina

3. Best Luxury Accommodations

Marrakech is home to some of the most luxurious hotels and riads in the world, offering opulent surroundings, world-class service, and an unforgettable experience. Whether you want to stay in a palatial riad, a five-star resort, or a high-end boutique hotel, these luxury accommodations will ensure a stay filled with indulgence and comfort.

**La Mamounia**
One of Marrakech's most iconic hotels, **La Mamounia** is the epitome of luxury and elegance. Set within lush gardens just outside the Medina, this five-star hotel has been a favorite of celebrities and royalty for decades. The hotel features lavishly decorated rooms and suites, a stunning spa with a traditional hammam, multiple gourmet restaurants, and expansive pools. Its blend of Moroccan design and Art Deco elements, along with

impeccable service, makes it one of the most sought-after luxury stays in Marrakech.

**Price Range**: $600–$1,500 per night

**Location**: Medina (near Jemaa el-Fnaa)

**Royal Mansour**
Commissioned by the King of Morocco, **Royal Mansour** is an ultra-luxurious hotel that offers an unparalleled experience in Marrakech. The property consists of private riads, each with its own courtyard, plunge pool, and butler service. Guests can enjoy the hotel's world-class spa, fine dining restaurants, and beautifully landscaped gardens. Royal Mansour is perfect for travelers looking for ultimate privacy, exclusivity, and indulgence.

**Price Range**: $1,000–$3,000 per night

**Location**: Medina

**Amanjena**
Part of the Aman Resorts collection, **Amanjena** is a peaceful luxury retreat located just outside Marrakech, near the Atlas Mountains. The resort features spacious **pavilions** and **villas** with private pools, surrounded by beautiful gardens and reflecting pools. Guests can enjoy a full range of wellness treatments at the Aman Spa, as well as fine dining at the resort's restaurants. Amanjena

is ideal for those seeking luxury and tranquility away from the city center.

**Price Range**: $800–$2,500 per night

**Location**: Outskirts of Marrakech

4. Other Noteworthy Accommodations

**Les Deux Tours**: A luxury boutique hotel set in a tranquil garden, offering private suites and villas with a blend of traditional and modern design.

**Price Range**: $250–$500 per night

**Location**: Palmeraie district

**El Fenn**: A boutique riad known for its chic decor, rooftop pool, and artistic atmosphere. It offers a luxurious stay with a focus on design and comfort.

**Price Range**: $300–$600 per night

**Location**: Medina

**Selman Marrakech**: A luxury hotel and equestrian estate that offers an extraordinary blend of Moroccan craftsmanship and opulent design.

**Price Range**: $600–$1,200 per night

**Location**: Route d'Amizmiz, Marrakech outskirts

A Stay for Every Style and Budget

Whether you're traveling on a budget, seeking mid-range comfort, or indulging in five-star luxury, Marrakech offers a diverse range of accommodations to suit every traveler. From traditional riads that immerse you in Moroccan culture to modern hotels with all the conveniences, the city provides endless options for a memorable stay. No matter where you choose to rest your head, Marrakech's legendary hospitality will ensure a warm welcome and a wonderful experience.

## Unique Stays: Camping, Villas, and Eco-Lodges

Marrakech is famous for its luxurious hotels and traditional riads, but for travelers looking for something a bit different, there are plenty of unique accommodations that offer a memorable stay. From desert camping under the stars to secluded villas surrounded by nature, and eco-lodges focused on sustainability, Marrakech provides a wide variety of one-of-a-kind experiences for adventurous travelers or those seeking a closer connection with nature.

## 1. Camping in the Agafay Desert

For a taste of the desert without traveling far from Marrakech, the **Agafay Desert** offers the perfect escape. Though it lacks the sandy dunes of the Sahara, the rocky, moon-like landscape is equally enchanting, especially at sunset. **Luxury desert camps**, also known as "glamping," offer a way to experience the beauty and serenity of the desert while still enjoying modern comforts.

**Scarabeo Camp**
Located about 45 minutes from Marrakech, **Scarabeo Camp** is a luxury desert camp that blends traditional nomadic living with a touch of elegance. The spacious canvas tents are outfitted with plush bedding, handcrafted furniture, and vintage lanterns, creating an atmosphere of rustic luxury. Guests can enjoy dinner under the stars, take camel rides, or relax by the campfire. Scarabeo Camp offers a peaceful escape into nature, with the dramatic backdrop of the **Atlas Mountains** visible in the distance.

**What to Expect**: Luxury tents with private bathrooms, traditional Moroccan meals, activities such as camel trekking and quad biking.

**Location**: Agafay Desert (45-minute drive from Marrakech)

**Inara Camp**

Another popular option for desert glamping, **Inara Camp** offers beautifully designed tents and a range of outdoor activities in the Agafay Desert. The camp is known for its intimate atmosphere, with each tent featuring a private terrace and stunning views of the surrounding landscape. Inara Camp also provides special experiences, such as candlelit dinners and guided stargazing, perfect for couples or those looking for a romantic desert retreat.

**What to Expect**: Luxurious tents, Moroccan cuisine, hammam, stargazing, and off-road adventures.

**Location**: Agafay Desert

2. Secluded Villas

For travelers seeking privacy and exclusivity, staying in a **private villa** offers the ultimate in luxury and tranquility. Marrakech is home to numerous villas, many located just outside the city or in the serene **Palmeraie district**. These villas are perfect for families, groups, or couples looking for their own personal retreat, complete with lush gardens, private pools, and dedicated staff.

**Villa K**

Located just outside the city center, **Villa K** is a modern, stylish villa with five bedrooms, a large swimming pool, and beautifully landscaped gardens. The villa's minimalist design blends contemporary architecture with Moroccan touches, offering guests a chic and peaceful stay. With a private chef, housekeeper, and concierge service, Villa K offers the luxury of a boutique hotel with the privacy of a private residence.

**What to Expect**: Private pool, dedicated staff, personalized meals, and a peaceful atmosphere.

**Location**: Just outside Marrakech

**Dar Ayniwen**
Set in the tranquil **Palmeraie district**, **Dar Ayniwen** is a luxury villa and boutique hotel surrounded by lush gardens and palm trees. The property offers a handful of individually designed suites and rooms, each with unique Moroccan decor. The villa features a large swimming pool, spa facilities, and even a private zoo, making it an ideal choice for families or those looking for a luxurious, nature-filled escape.

**What to Expect**: Pool, spa, gardens, zoo, and high-end services, including private chauffeurs and chefs.

**Location**: Palmeraie district

**Villa des Orangers**
A member of the prestigious **Relais & Châteaux** group, **Villa des Orangers** is an elegant riad-style villa located

in the heart of the Medina. With just 27 rooms and suites, the villa offers a boutique hotel experience with the privacy of a villa. The property features traditional Moroccan decor, three swimming pools, a rooftop terrace, and a luxury spa, creating a tranquil oasis within the bustling city.

**What to Expect**: Intimate riad-style atmosphere, spa, rooftop terrace, gourmet dining, and personalized service.

**Location**: Medina, Marrakech

3. Eco-Lodges and Sustainable Stays

For environmentally conscious travelers, Marrakech and its surrounding areas offer **eco-lodges** that focus on sustainability and responsible tourism. These lodges are often located in more remote areas, surrounded by natural beauty, and designed to have minimal impact on the environment. Many eco-lodges use renewable energy, source local ingredients for meals, and incorporate traditional building techniques that respect the environment.

**Kasbah Bab Ourika**
Perched on a hilltop in the **Ourika Valley**, **Kasbah Bab Ourika** is an eco-lodge that offers breathtaking views of the **Atlas Mountains** and the surrounding olive groves

and orange orchards. The kasbah is built using traditional Berber techniques and is powered by renewable energy. Guests can enjoy organic meals made from locally sourced ingredients, explore the nearby villages and valleys, or relax in the eco-friendly infinity pool.

**What to Expect**: Eco-friendly construction, organic meals, infinity pool, and hiking in the Atlas Mountains.

**Location**: Ourika Valley (45-minute drive from Marrakech)

**Terre des Étoiles**
An eco-lodge located in the Agafay Desert, **Terre des Étoiles** offers a unique blend of desert camping and sustainability. The camp features luxurious eco-friendly tents, all designed to minimize their environmental impact. The lodge promotes sustainability through its use of solar energy and water conservation practices. Guests can enjoy activities such as camel trekking, yoga, and stargazing, all while experiencing the beauty of the desert in an eco-conscious setting.

**What to Expect**: Eco-friendly tents, solar energy, Moroccan cuisine, and sustainable practices.

**Location**: Agafay Desert

**Douar Samra**

Located in the stunning **Imlil Valley** at the base of Mount Toubkal, **Douar Samra** is an eco-lodge offering a rustic yet charming retreat in the High Atlas Mountains. The lodge is set in a traditional Berber house and is run by a local family who emphasize sustainable living and cultural exchange. Guests can enjoy simple, wholesome meals, explore the nearby hiking trails, and experience the warmth of Berber hospitality in a beautiful mountain setting.

**What to Expect**: Traditional Berber hospitality, rustic charm, organic meals, and guided hikes.

**Location**: Imlil Valley, Atlas Mountains

4. Best Time to Experience Unique Stays

The best time to enjoy these unique accommodations in Marrakech depends on your travel preferences:

**Camping and Desert Stays**: The best time for desert camping in the Agafay is during the cooler months, from **October to May**, when daytime temperatures are comfortable, and evenings are cool.

**Villas**: Villas are a great option year-round, though the summer months (**June to August**) can be quite hot, especially in the city. Spring and fall offer the best weather for outdoor activities.

**Eco-Lodges**: For mountain eco-lodges like **Kasbah Bab Ourika** and **Douar Samra**, the best time to visit is during **spring (March to May)** and **fall (September to November)**, when the weather is mild, and the landscape is lush.

## Unique Stays for Unforgettable Experiences

Whether you're camping under the stars in the Agafay Desert, relaxing in a private villa, or retreating to a sustainable eco-lodge in the Atlas Mountains, Marrakech offers a variety of unique accommodations that cater to every traveler's desire for adventure, luxury, and connection to nature. These experiences allow you to explore Morocco's diverse landscapes and cultures while enjoying the comforts and beauty of your surroundings.

Marrakech is famous for its luxurious hotels and traditional riads, but for travelers looking for something a bit different, there are plenty of unique accommodations that offer a memorable stay. From desert camping under the stars to secluded villas surrounded by nature, and eco-lodges focused on sustainability, Marrakech provides a wide variety of one-of-a-kind experiences for adventurous travelers or those seeking a closer connection with nature.

1. Camping in the Agafay Desert

For a taste of the desert without traveling far from Marrakech, the **Agafay Desert** offers the perfect escape. Though it lacks the sandy dunes of the Sahara, the rocky, moon-like landscape is equally enchanting, especially at sunset. **Luxury desert camps**, also known as "glamping," offer a way to experience the beauty and serenity of the desert while still enjoying modern comforts.

**Scarabeo Camp**
Located about 45 minutes from Marrakech, **Scarabeo Camp** is a luxury desert camp that blends traditional nomadic living with a touch of elegance. The spacious canvas tents are outfitted with plush bedding, handcrafted furniture, and vintage lanterns, creating an atmosphere of rustic luxury. Guests can enjoy dinner under the stars, take camel rides, or relax by the campfire. Scarabeo Camp offers a peaceful escape into nature, with the dramatic backdrop of the **Atlas Mountains** visible in the distance.

**What to Expect**: Luxury tents with private bathrooms, traditional Moroccan meals, activities such as camel trekking and quad biking.

**Location**: Agafay Desert (45-minute drive from Marrakech)

**Inara Camp**

Another popular option for desert glamping, **Inara Camp** offers beautifully designed tents and a range of outdoor activities in the Agafay Desert. The camp is known for its intimate atmosphere, with each tent featuring a private terrace and stunning views of the surrounding landscape. Inara Camp also provides special experiences, such as candlelit dinners and guided stargazing, perfect for couples or those looking for a romantic desert retreat.

**What to Expect**: Luxurious tents, Moroccan cuisine, hammam, stargazing, and off-road adventures.

**Location**: Agafay Desert

2. Secluded Villas

For travelers seeking privacy and exclusivity, staying in a **private villa** offers the ultimate in luxury and tranquility. Marrakech is home to numerous villas, many located just outside the city or in the serene **Palmeraie district**. These villas are perfect for families, groups, or couples looking for their own personal retreat, complete with lush gardens, private pools, and dedicated staff.

**Villa K**

Located just outside the city center, **Villa K** is a modern, stylish villa with five bedrooms, a large swimming pool, and beautifully landscaped gardens. The villa's minimalist design blends contemporary architecture with Moroccan touches, offering guests a chic and peaceful stay. With a private chef, housekeeper, and concierge service, Villa K offers the luxury of a boutique hotel with the privacy of a private residence.

**What to Expect**: Private pool, dedicated staff, personalized meals, and a peaceful atmosphere.

**Location**: Just outside Marrakech

**Dar Ayniwen**

Set in the tranquil **Palmeraie district**, **Dar Ayniwen** is a luxury villa and boutique hotel surrounded by lush gardens and palm trees. The property offers a handful of individually designed suites and rooms, each with unique Moroccan decor. The villa features a large swimming pool, spa facilities, and even a private zoo, making it an ideal choice for families or those looking for a luxurious, nature-filled escape.

**What to Expect**: Pool, spa, gardens, zoo, and high-end services, including private chauffeurs and chefs.

**Location**: Palmeraie district

**Villa des Orangers**

A member of the prestigious **Relais & Châteaux** group, **Villa des Orangers** is an elegant riad-style villa located in the heart of the Medina. With just 27 rooms and suites, the villa offers a boutique hotel experience with the privacy of a villa. The property features traditional Moroccan decor, three swimming pools, a rooftop terrace, and a luxury spa, creating a tranquil oasis within the bustling city.

**What to Expect**: Intimate riad-style atmosphere, spa, rooftop terrace, gourmet dining, and personalized service.

**Location**: Medina, Marrakech

3. Eco-Lodges and Sustainable Stays

For environmentally conscious travelers, Marrakech and its surrounding areas offer **eco-lodges** that focus on sustainability and responsible tourism. These lodges are often located in more remote areas, surrounded by natural beauty, and designed to have minimal impact on the environment. Many eco-lodges use renewable energy, source local ingredients for meals, and incorporate traditional building techniques that respect the environment.

### Kasbah Bab Ourika

Perched on a hilltop in the **Ourika Valley**, **Kasbah Bab Ourika** is an eco-lodge that offers breathtaking views of the **Atlas Mountains** and the surrounding olive groves and orange orchards. The kasbah is built using traditional Berber techniques and is powered by renewable energy. Guests can enjoy organic meals made from locally sourced ingredients, explore the nearby villages and valleys, or relax in the eco-friendly infinity pool.

**What to Expect**: Eco-friendly construction, organic meals, infinity pool, and hiking in the Atlas Mountains.

**Location**: Ourika Valley (45-minute drive from Marrakech)

### Terre des Étoiles

An eco-lodge located in the Agafay Desert, **Terre des Étoiles** offers a unique blend of desert camping and sustainability. The camp features luxurious eco-friendly tents, all designed to minimize their environmental impact. The lodge promotes sustainability through its use of solar energy and water conservation practices. Guests can enjoy activities such as camel trekking, yoga, and stargazing, all while experiencing the beauty of the desert in an eco-conscious setting.

**What to Expect**: Eco-friendly tents, solar energy, Moroccan cuisine, and sustainable practices.

**Location**: Agafay Desert

**Douar Samra**
Located in the stunning **Imlil Valley** at the base of Mount Toubkal, **Douar Samra** is an eco-lodge offering a rustic yet charming retreat in the High Atlas Mountains. The lodge is set in a traditional Berber house and is run by a local family who emphasize sustainable living and cultural exchange. Guests can enjoy simple, wholesome meals, explore the nearby hiking trails, and experience the warmth of Berber hospitality in a beautiful mountain setting.

**What to Expect**: Traditional Berber hospitality, rustic charm, organic meals, and guided hikes.

**Location**: Imlil Valley, Atlas Mountains

4. Best Time to Experience Unique Stays

The best time to enjoy these unique accommodations in Marrakech depends on your travel preferences:

**Camping and Desert Stays**: The best time for desert camping in the Agafay is during the cooler months, from **October to May**, when daytime temperatures are comfortable, and evenings are cool.

**Villas**: Villas are a great option year-round, though the summer months (**June to August**) can be quite hot, especially in the city. Spring and fall offer the best weather for outdoor activities.

**Eco-Lodges**: For mountain eco-lodges like **Kasbah Bab Ourika** and **Douar Samra**, the best time to visit is during **spring (March to May)** and **fall (September to November)**, when the weather is mild, and the landscape is lush.

Unique Stays for Unforgettable Experiences

Whether you're camping under the stars in the Agafay Desert, relaxing in a private villa, or retreating to a sustainable eco-lodge in the Atlas Mountains, Marrakech offers a variety of unique accommodations that cater to every traveler's desire for adventure, luxury, and connection to nature. These experiences allow you to explore Morocco's diverse landscapes and cultures while enjoying the comforts and beauty of your surroundings.

# Essential Travel Tips

## Navigating the City: Transportation Options and Taxis

of the Medina and the wider, more modern streets of neighborhoods like Gueliz and Hivernage, getting around the city requires a little planning. Luckily, Marrakech offers several transportation options to suit every traveler's needs, from taxis and buses to more unique forms of transport like **calèches** (horse-drawn carriages). This guide will help you understand the best ways to get around and offer tips for using taxis, which are one of the most common and convenient forms of transport in the city.

1. Walking in the Medina

The **Medina** of Marrakech is best explored on foot. The narrow, winding streets and bustling souks make it a pedestrian-friendly area, though it can also be confusing for newcomers. Be prepared to get a little lost, as the Medina is a maze of alleys, many of which are unmarked. However, wandering through these streets is part of the charm, and there are plenty of shops, cafés, and landmarks to stop at along the way.

**Navigating Tip**: To avoid getting too lost, use landmarks like the **Jemaa el-Fna** square and the **Koutoubia**

**Mosque** as reference points. Maps on your phone can help, but in Medina, even Google Maps may struggle to keep up. If you do get lost, locals are usually helpful in pointing you in the right direction.

**Safety Note**: Be cautious when walking in the evening, especially in less busy parts of the Medina. Stick to well-lit areas and avoid walking alone late at night.

2. Taxis in Marrakech

Taxis are one of the most popular and convenient ways to get around Marrakech, especially if you're traveling between neighborhoods or outside the Medina. There are two types of taxis in Marrakech: **petit taxis** and **grand taxis**. Understanding the differences between them and knowing how to use them can make your travels much smoother.

**Petit Taxis**:
**Petit taxis** are small, metered taxis that are ideal for short trips within Marrakech. They are typically beige in color and can accommodate up to three passengers. These taxis are perfect for getting around the city's main neighborhoods, including the Medina, Gueliz, and Hivernage.

**How to Use**: Always ask the driver to turn on the **meter** (compteur) when you get in the taxi. If the driver refuses to use the meter, negotiate a price before starting your journey. It's best to know the approximate fare in advance (ask your hotel or a local) to avoid overpaying. Petit taxis are generally inexpensive, with fares ranging from 10 to 20 MAD ($1–$2 USD) for short trips around the city.

**Important Tip**: Petit taxis are not allowed to leave Marrakech's city limits. If you're planning to go outside the city, such as to the **Agafay Desert** or the **Palmeraie**, you'll need to use a grand taxi.

**Grand Taxis**:
**Grand taxis** are larger, usually older cars (often Mercedes) that can carry up to six passengers. These taxis are typically used for longer trips outside the city or for journeys to places like the airport, nearby towns, or the desert.

**How to Use**: Grand taxis don't use meters, so you'll need to negotiate the fare before starting your journey. Fares depend on the distance and number of passengers. For trips like going to the **Menara Airport** or **Ourika Valley**, grand taxis are the best option.

**Tip**: If you're traveling alone or with a small group, you can either pay for the whole taxi or wait for other passengers to fill the remaining seats to reduce the cost.

3. Other Forms of Transportation

While taxis are the most common way to get around, Marrakech offers a few other transport options that can be useful, depending on your needs.

**Buses**:
Marrakech has a network of city buses that are a cheap way to get around, though they can be crowded and less convenient for tourists unfamiliar with the routes. The bus system is managed by **Alsa**, and tickets cost around 4 MAD ($0.40 USD) per journey. Buses are most useful if you're traveling to outer districts like **Gueliz** or to the **Palmeraie** area.

**Bus Tip**: Bus routes and schedules can be hard to find online, so ask your hotel or a local for advice if you plan to use them.

**Calèches (Horse-Drawn Carriages)**:
For a more scenic and leisurely way to explore Marrakech, you can take a ride in a **calèche**. These horse-drawn carriages are popular with tourists and offer a relaxed way to see the city's main sights. Calèches are often found near **Jemaa el-Fnaa** and **Koutoubia Mosque**, and they typically offer rides around Medina, the **Menara Gardens**, and the **Majorelle Gardens**.

**How to Use**: Agree on the price before starting your ride. Prices can vary depending on the length of the tour and your negotiating skills, but a typical one-hour ride costs around 150 to 200 MAD ($15–$20 USD).

**Bicycles and Motorbikes**:
Renting a **bicycle** or **motorbike** is another option for those who prefer more independent exploration. Many hotels and rental shops in Gueliz and Hivernage offer bike rentals. While it can be an enjoyable way to get around, the traffic in Marrakech can be chaotic, especially in the Medina, so only confident riders should attempt to navigate the city by bike or motorbike.

4. Airport Transfers

The **Menara Airport** (RAK) is located just a few kilometers from the city center, and there are several options for getting to and from the airport.

**Taxis**:
Taking a taxi is the most common and convenient way to reach the city from the airport. **Grand taxis** are available outside the terminal, and the fare to the Medina or Gueliz should be negotiated before departure. Expect to pay between 100 and 150 MAD ($10–$15 USD), depending on your bargaining skills and the time of day.

**Shuttle Buses**:

**Alsa** operates a shuttle bus (Bus No. 19) between the airport and the city center, with stops in Gueliz, Hivernage, and Jemaa el-Fnaa. The fare is around 30 MAD ($3 USD) for a one-way trip. The bus runs every 30 minutes during peak times and is a good option if you're traveling light and want an affordable alternative to taxis.

5. Navigating Marrakech with Confidence

Getting around Marrakech can feel overwhelming at first, especially with the city's bustling streets and lively traffic. However, by knowing your transportation options and following these simple tips, you'll quickly get the hang of navigating the city like a local.

**Taxi Tip**: Always carry small bills, as taxi drivers often claim not to have change. It's also helpful to ask a local or your hotel about typical fares for your destination, so you have an idea of what you should pay.

**Language Tip**: Most taxi drivers speak Arabic and French. If you don't speak these languages, it's helpful to have your destination written down or use Google Maps to show the driver where you're headed.

**Peak Hours**: Traffic can be heavy in Marrakech, particularly during rush hours (around 8–9 AM and 5–7

PM). If you need to travel during these times, be prepared for longer travel times.

## Choosing the Right Transport for Your Trip

Whether you're walking through the winding streets of the Medina, hopping in a taxi to visit the new city, or taking a scenic ride in a horse-drawn carriage, Marrakech offers a variety of ways to explore its vibrant neighborhoods. By understanding the different transportation options available, you'll be able to navigate the city with ease and make the most of your time in this captivating destination

## Safety and Scams to Avoid

Marrakech is a vibrant and welcoming city that draws travelers from all over the world with its rich culture, bustling markets, and historic sites. While the city is generally safe for tourists, it's important to be aware of certain safety tips and common scams to avoid while exploring. By staying vigilant and knowing what to look out for, you can ensure your trip is smooth and enjoyable.

1. General Safety Tips

Marrakech is considered a safe destination for travelers, but as with any major city, it's important to take basic precautions, especially when navigating the busy streets and markets.

**Watch Your Belongings**: In crowded areas like the **Medina**, **Jemaa el-Fnaa**, and the **souks**, be mindful of your belongings. Petty theft, such as pickpocketing, can occur, especially in busy places. Keep your valuables close, preferably in a money belt or an anti-theft bag. Avoid keeping items like your phone or wallet in your back pocket.

**Avoid Dark, Isolated Areas at Night**: While the Medina is generally safe, some narrow alleys can feel isolated at night. Stick to well-lit, busy streets after dark, and avoid wandering alone in quiet areas. If you're staying in a riad, ask the staff for directions and advice on safe routes back to your accommodation.

**Respect Local Customs**: Morocco is a predominantly Muslim country, and it's important to respect local customs, especially in terms of dress. While Marrakech is more relaxed than other parts of the country, dressing modestly (especially for women) can help you avoid unwanted attention. Cover your shoulders, knees, and avoid revealing clothing when exploring the city.

**Keep Small Bills for Taxis and Shops**: It's common for taxi drivers, shopkeepers, and market vendors to claim they don't have change, which can lead to you overpaying. Always carry small bills (such as 10 and 20 MAD) for transactions to avoid this issue.

2. Common Scams in Marrakech

As a popular tourist destination, Marrakech has its share of scams, especially in tourist-heavy areas like **Jemaa el-Fnaa** and the souks. Being aware of these common scams will help you navigate the city with confidence.

**The "Helpful Guide" Scam**: In Medina, especially near popular landmarks, you may encounter people offering to guide you through the souks or to a specific destination. While some guides are legitimate, others may lead you in circles or to shops where they'll pressure you to buy something. Once you reach your destination, they may demand a large tip for their "services."

**How to Avoid**: Politely decline offers of unsolicited help. If you need assistance, ask someone working at your accommodation for directions or hire a licensed guide from a trusted source.

**Fake Tourist Information**: Sometimes, scammers will stand near attractions or riads and claim that certain places are closed or that your route is blocked. They may then offer to guide you to a different place, often a shop or business that pays them a commission.

**How to Avoid**: Always double-check information with official sources or your hotel. Attractions in Marrakech generally have regular hours and are rarely closed unexpectedly.

**Overcharging in Souks**: Haggling is a common practice in the souks, but sometimes shopkeepers may try to overcharge tourists, especially if you're unfamiliar with the typical prices of goods like spices, leather products, or textiles.

**How to Avoid**: Always haggle politely but firmly, and don't be afraid to walk away if the price is too high. It helps to ask your hotel staff for guidance on fair prices before you go shopping. Remember, haggling is part of the culture, so approach it with a sense of fun and curiosity.

**Fake Products**: In some markets, you might be offered "genuine" products, such as **argan oil**, **saffron**, or **leather goods**, which turn out to be fake or poor quality.

**How to Avoid**: Purchase goods from reputable stores or cooperatives, especially for items like argan oil or spices. If something seems too good to be true, it probably is.

Authentic argan oil is usually more expensive, and saffron should not be sold at rock-bottom prices.

**Henna Scams**: In **Jemaa el-Fnaa**, you'll find many women offering to give you a **henna tattoo**. Some will begin applying henna without asking, and then demand an exorbitant fee when they're finished. The quality of the henna may also be poor, with some using chemicals that can irritate the skin.

**How to Avoid**: Politely decline if you're not interested in getting henna. If you want a henna tattoo, go to a reputable henna artist recommended by your hotel or one you research in advance.

**Street Performers and Photos**: Jemaa el-Fnaa is known for its lively street performers, including **snake charmers**, **musicians**, and **monkey handlers**. While taking photos of these performers is tempting, many performers will aggressively demand payment after you take a picture, often asking for far more than expected.

**How to Avoid**: Always ask for permission before taking a photo, and agree on a price beforehand. It's common to give 10–20 MAD for a photo, but some performers may ask for more, so make sure you clarify before snapping a picture.

**Taxis Without Meters**: As mentioned in the transportation section, some taxi drivers in Marrakech may try to overcharge tourists by not using the meter or by quoting an inflated price at the end of the ride.

**How to Avoid**: Always insist on using the meter when you get into a **petit taxi**, or agree on the fare before you begin your journey. If the driver refuses to use the meter, politely exit the taxi and find another one.

3. What to Do If You Get Scammed

If you do fall victim to a scam, the best approach is to stay calm and avoid escalating the situation. Most scams in Marrakech are minor and can be resolved with a polite but firm response.

**Be Firm**: If someone is pressuring you to pay for a service you didn't ask for, remain polite but stand your ground. Let them know you won't pay for something you didn't request, and walk away if necessary.

**Report to Your Hotel**: If you experience an issue, let your hotel staff know. They can often help you avoid future scams, recommend trustworthy services, and offer advice on how to handle specific situations.

**Call for Help**: In case of more serious issues, you can contact the local **tourist police**. They are stationed near major tourist attractions and are there to help visitors resolve disputes or report scams.

4. Currency and Payment Safety

Marrakech operates primarily on a **cash economy**, especially in the souks and smaller shops, though credit cards are accepted in larger establishments and luxury hotels.

**ATM Tips**: Use ATMs inside banks or reputable hotels to avoid tampering or scams. Be cautious when withdrawing large sums of money, and store your cash in a secure place like a money belt.

**Avoid Overpaying**: Some shops or restaurants may give incorrect change, either by accident or intentionally. Always count your change carefully, and don't hesitate to point out mistakes politely.

5. Dealing with Street Hassle

In tourist-heavy areas like the Medina and Jemaa el-Fnaa, you'll likely be approached by vendors, street performers, and guides offering services. While this is part of the lively atmosphere of Marrakech, it can sometimes feel overwhelming.

**Polite Decline**: The best way to handle unwanted offers is with a polite but firm "no, thank you" ("la, shukran" in

Arabic) and continue walking. Most vendors will respect your response and move on.

**Stay Confident**: Walk with purpose, and don't stop to engage in conversation if you're not interested in a service or product. The more confident you appear, the less likely you are to be hassled.

Staying Safe in Marrakech

Marrakech is an exciting and welcoming city, and with a little caution and awareness, you can enjoy your visit without any issues. By understanding common scams and following basic safety tips, you'll be able to navigate the bustling streets and markets with confidence Packing for Marrakech requires a balance between practicality and respect for local customs. The city's unique blend of culture, climate, and environment means that travelers should be prepared for a range of experiences—e. Remember to stay alert, but also embrace the city's energy and warmth, and you'll leave with wonderful memories.

## Packing Essentials for Marrakech

from wandering the bustling souks to relaxing at a rooftop café or exploring the nearby desert. This guide will help you pack wisely, ensuring you're comfortable and well-prepared for your trip.

1. Clothing Essentials

Marrakech's climate can be hot during the day, especially in the summer, but cool in the evenings and mornings, especially during winter months. Packing versatile, breathable clothing is key, along with items that respect the more conservative dress codes in Morocco.

**Lightweight, Breathable Fabrics**: Marrakech can get very hot, particularly during the summer months (June to August), so pack clothing made from lightweight, breathable materials like **cotton** or **linen**. Loose-fitting clothing will help you stay cool in the heat and provide comfort while exploring the city.

**Modest Clothing**: Morocco is a predominantly Muslim country, and while Marrakech is more liberal than other cities, it's important to dress modestly, especially when visiting the Medina, mosques, or other cultural sites. Women should pack **long skirts or dresses**, **loose pants**, and **tops that cover the shoulders and chest**. Men should also opt for **lightweight pants** or **long shorts**, along with t-shirts or button-up shirts that cover the shoulders.

**Tip**: A lightweight **scarf** is useful for both men and women. It can provide extra coverage when needed, offer sun protection, or serve as a stylish accessory.

**Layers for Evenings**: Even in the warmer months, Marrakech's evenings can cool down, especially from November to March. Pack a **light sweater**, **cardigan**, or **jacket** to stay warm once the sun goes down.

**Comfortable Walking Shoes**: The Medina's narrow alleys and cobbled streets mean you'll likely be walking a lot. Pack comfortable, sturdy shoes such as **sneakers**, **sandals with good support**, or **lightweight hiking shoes** if you plan to explore areas outside the city.

2. Sun Protection

The Moroccan sun can be intense, especially during the summer. Protecting yourself from sunburn and dehydration is crucial, whether you're exploring the city or venturing into the nearby desert.

**Sunscreen**: Pack high-SPF **sunscreen** (50+ SPF) to protect your skin from the strong UV rays. Make sure to bring enough, as sunscreen can be expensive in tourist areas.

**Wide-Brimmed Hat**: A **wide-brimmed hat** or **cap** will help shield your face, neck, and shoulders from the sun while adding an extra layer of protection.

**Sunglasses**: A pair of **good-quality sunglasses** is essential for protecting your eyes from the bright sun, especially when visiting open markets or the desert.

**Reusable Water Bottle**: Staying hydrated is crucial in Marrakech's heat. Bring a **reusable water bottle** that you can fill up throughout the day to reduce plastic waste and ensure you always have water on hand.

3. Toiletries and Personal Care

Marrakech's heat and dry climate can be tough on your skin and hair, so it's essential to pack the right toiletries to stay fresh and comfortable.

**Moisturizer**: The dry climate can be harsh on your skin, so pack a good **moisturizer** to keep your skin hydrated. You might also want to bring a **hydrating facial mist** for a refreshing boost during the day.

**Lip Balm**: A **hydrating lip balm** with SPF is essential, as the dry air and sun can quickly dry out your lips.

**Hair Care**: Bring **shampoo** and **conditioner** that suit your hair type, as the local water can be harder on your hair than what you're used to. For longer stays, consider packing a **deep conditioner** or **leave-in treatment** to combat the effects of the dry air.

**Hand Sanitizer and Wet Wipes**: The bustling streets and markets can be dusty, and access to soap isn't always guaranteed in public restrooms. **Hand sanitizer** and **wet wipes** are useful for freshening up on the go.

**Toilet Paper/Tissues**: Public restrooms in Morocco often do not provide toilet paper, so it's a good idea to carry a small pack of **tissues** or toilet paper with you.

4. Travel Accessories

Packing a few key travel accessories will make your trip to Marrakech more convenient and comfortable.

**Crossbody Bag or Backpack**: A secure **crossbody bag** or small **backpack** with zippered compartments is ideal for carrying your essentials while exploring the city. Choose a bag that's lightweight, comfortable, and can be worn close to your body for added security.

**Money Belt or Anti-Theft Wallet**: In busy areas like Jemaa el-Fnaa and the souks, a **money belt** or **anti-theft wallet** can help keep your cash, cards, and passport safe from pickpockets.

**Portable Charger**: With so much to see and do, your phone battery may drain quickly from taking photos and using maps. Bring a **portable charger** to ensure your devices stay powered throughout the day.

**Plug Adapter**: Morocco uses **Type C and E** plugs, with a voltage of 220V. If you're traveling from a country that uses a different plug type, pack a **universal adapter** to charge your devices.

**Language App or Phrasebook**: While many people in Marrakech speak French or some English, knowing a few basic phrases in **Arabic** or **French** can be helpful and appreciated. Consider downloading a **language app** or bringing a small **phrasebook** to assist with communication.

5. Specific Items for Desert Excursions

If you're planning to visit the **Agafay Desert** or venture farther to the **Sahara**, there are a few additional items you'll want to pack to ensure your comfort during your desert adventure.

**Lightweight Scarf or Shawl**: A large scarf, like a **shemagh** or **pashmina**, can be used to protect your face and neck from sand and sun while traveling through the desert.

**Loose, Long Clothing**: In the desert, wearing **loose, long-sleeved** clothing can protect you from the sun and sand while keeping you cool. Breathable fabrics like cotton or linen are best.

**Sturdy Footwear**: If you're planning on walking or hiking in the desert, pack comfortable **closed-toe shoes** like lightweight boots or hiking shoes to protect your feet from the sand and heat.

**Headlamp or Flashlight**: If you're staying overnight in the desert, a **headlamp** or small **flashlight** can be useful for navigating campsites after dark.

6. Health and Safety Items

Marrakech is a safe destination, but it's always smart to pack a few essential health and safety items to keep you prepared for any situation.

**Basic First-Aid Kit**: Pack a small **first-aid kit** with essentials like **band-aids, antiseptic wipes, pain relievers**, and any prescription medications you may need during your trip.

**Insect Repellent**: While mosquitoes aren't a major problem in Marrakech, it's a good idea to bring **insect repellent**, especially if you're planning to visit rural areas or the desert.

**Imodium or Anti-Diarrheal Medication**: Moroccan food is delicious but can be rich and unfamiliar to some visitors, leading to digestive issues. Bringing **Imodium** or other anti-diarrheal medication can be helpful in case of an upset stomach.

**Rehydration Salts**: If you're traveling during the hotter months, **oral rehydration salts** can help you stay hydrated and replace electrolytes lost due to sweating.

7. Documents and Important Information

Ensure you have all the necessary documents and travel information ready before your trip.

**Passport and Photocopies**: Always carry your **passport**, and keep a **photocopy** of it in a separate location in case the original is lost. Some accommodations may require a copy for check-in.

**Travel Insurance**: Make sure you have **travel insurance** that covers health emergencies, lost luggage, and trip cancellations. Carry a copy of your policy details and emergency contact numbers.

**Emergency Contacts**: Have a list of **emergency contacts**, including the local embassy, your hotel, and any tour operators.

Packing for a Comfortable and Enjoyable Stay

By packing the right clothing, accessories, and essentials for your trip to Marrakech, you'll be well-prepared to explore the city and surrounding areas in comfort and style. Whether you're wandering through the souks, relaxing at a riad, or embarking on a desert adventure, thoughtful packing will help you make the most of your time in this fascinating destination.

## A Journey to Remember

Marrakech is a city like no other, where ancient traditions blend seamlessly with modern influences, and where every corner offers something new to discover. From the bustling souks and historic landmarks of the Medina to the serene beauty of the nearby desert and mountains, Marrakech captivates visitors with its vibrant energy, rich culture, and stunning landscapes.

Whether you've come for the world-class cuisine, the shopping, the adventure, or simply to immerse yourself in the sensory delights of this dynamic city, there's no doubt that Marrakech leaves a lasting impression. The city's warm hospitality, diverse experiences, and unique charm ensure that every traveler finds something to love here.

As you leave Marrakech, you'll take with you more than just memories of the sights, sounds, and tastes. The experiences you've had—whether it was sipping mint tea in a quiet riad courtyard, haggling in the souks, exploring ancient palaces, or riding a camel across the Agafay Desert—will stay with you long after your journey ends.

No matter how long or short your stay, Marrakech has a way of drawing you back. The city's intoxicating blend of old and new, tranquility and excitement, promises that there's always more to explore, more to learn, and more to experience. We hope this guide has provided you with the insights and inspiration you need to make the most of your trip, and that it will serve as a useful companion as you navigate the wonders of Marrakech.

Safe travels, and may your time in this extraordinary city be as magical as the stories it holds.

Printed in Great Britain
by Amazon